BACKYARD GARDENING

ALL THE BASICS YOU NEED TO KNOW TO START
AND SUSTAIN A SELF-SUFFICIENT THRIVING
ORGANIC VEGETABLE GARDEN EVEN IF YOU ARE A
BEGINNER GARDENER

PETER GREENFIELD

© **Copyright 2020 - All rights reserved.**

The content contained within this book may not be reproduced, duplicated, or transmitted without direct written permission from the author or the publisher.

Under no circumstances will any blame or legal responsibility be held against the publisher, or author, for any damages, reparation, or monetary loss due to the information contained within this book, either directly or indirectly.

Legal Notice:

This book is copyright protected. It is only for personal use. You cannot amend, distribute, sell, use, quote, or paraphrase any part of this book, without the consent of the author or publisher.

Disclaimer Notice:

Please note, the information contained within this document is for educational and entertainment purposes only. All effort has been executed to present accurate, up to date, reliable, complete information. No warranties of any kind are declared or implied. Readers acknowledge that the author is not engaged in the rendering of legal, financial, medical, or professional advice. The content within this book has been derived from various sources. Please consult a licensed professional before attempting any techniques outlined in this book.

By reading this document, the reader agrees that under no circumstances is the author responsible for any losses, direct or indirect, that are incurred as a result of the use of the information contained within this document, including, but not limited to, errors, omissions, or inaccuracies.

CONTENTS

Introduction   5

1. Organic Farming   7
2. Nourish to Flourish   18
3. Pest and Disease Control   42
4. Weed Management   73
5. Choosing Your Crop   87
6. Getting You Started   111

Conclusion   133
References   137

A Free Gift Just for You!

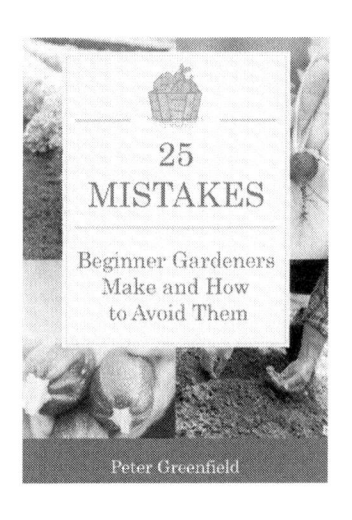

Download this free ebook to ensure you are not making any of those mistakes that could jeopardize your hard work. Click the link below.

Do not start your garden without reading this ebook. Download the Free ebook

https://bit.ly/25-mistakes

Want access to a private community of passionate gardeners?

Being around like-minded people is the first step in being successful at gardening.

Join us and be part of an amazing community of gardeners just like you and share your experiences, stories, pictures and questions.

JOIN US!
https://bit.ly/backyardGardenerCommunity

INTRODUCTION

Organic farming has become popular all over the world, and while some people are satisfied with buying organic products from the store, others need even more control over what is served on their plates. Organic gardeners are becoming more and more present in the United States, Europe, and Australia. Each continent comes with its own perks and disadvantages when it comes to agriculture. They are so different in climate, wildlife, and variety of available plants that grow. However, somehow, they manage to complement each other.

Organic farmers from all over the world share experiences, invent new ways of working the soil, more productive systems of irrigation, or simply better and safer pest control methods. This shared experience is pushing the industry forward, allowing new ideas to come true and making organic gardening available to everyone who has a small backyard.

No matter the size of your garden, the challenges will be there, and with the help of this book, you will not only learn how to start your own garden but also how to overcome the daily challenges of your new favorite hobby. Yes, gardening starts as a hobby for many of us, and for a lot of people, it remains just that. A small backyard garden doesn't require much work, and even those with busy schedules are able to dive into it. There are planting methods that will allow you to enjoy your small organic garden without having to worry about weed control or soil fertility.

And then there are those who find their true purpose in organic gardening. Those are the kind of people who feel the call of the earth, nature, and the nurturing instincts of their own. These people thrive when working in their gardens, and over time, they tend to extend them. Soon after, they grow into real organic farmers with acres and acres of arable land which will produce not just for their families, but for the whole community. Who knows, maybe you will discover that you are one of those people just by reading the pages of this book.

ORGANIC FARMING

When chemical and synthetic fertilizers and pesticides were first introduced, farmers were overjoyed at the sight of their massively improved yields. Keep in mind that during those early days when chemicals were first introduced into farming, nobody really noticed the downsides of using them. The soil and ecosystem were healthy and seemed to be unaffected. It was a new milestone in modern agriculture that meant more easily accessible food at lower prices. But then why all the talk about organic farming like in the days before this agricultural revolution?

As the decades past, we were finally exposed to the long-term devastation that was being caused by the new conventional farming methods. The soil started degrading, underground water supplies became toxic for human and animal consumption, and wildlife became sick or worse. We now have decades worth of data and we can clearly see how the bee population significantly declined over time since the introduction of chemical pesticides, and how the environment overall slowly entered in a state of decay.

As a result of all these issues that came to light, new organic farming techniques were developed to work with the old ones and try to live in balance with the plant and animal life surrounding us. The general idea behind this farming style is that we rely on methods that don't involve the use of synthetic or poisonous materials that negatively affect the ecosystem. Only biological products are used in responsible quantities to maintain the soil's fertility and repel pests naturally without damaging other fauna and flora. In other words, the point of organic farming is to keep pollution and waste at a bare minimum and nurture our food crops without causing damage to human, animal, and plant life alike. Genetically modified organisms (GMOs) are also banned from being used in organic farming because we don't know the long-term effects of consuming such products.

All organic farming relies on classic agriculture methodologies that include organic waste, non-chemical pest control, crop rotation, mineral additives, and natural fertilizers.

CONVENTIONAL VS. ORGANIC

Conventional farming methods involve several processes that are damaging to the environment, and the problems already start with the preparation of the farmland.

A conventional farmer won't begin by planting seeds. The first step is to treat the land with various chemical products in order to wipe out the encroaching nature that fills his piece of land and eliminate most insects and fungi in addition to the native plants. Furthermore, future farmland is going to be fertilized with petroleum products. On the other hand, we have the organic farmer that starts by fertilizing the land using only organic fertilizers like bone meal and manure.

Next, the conventional farmer treats the seeds with pesticides and fungicides to prevent any pests from eating them. Sometimes, various chemical repellents are added to the water that is used to irrigate the plants. The purpose of this 'enhanced' water is to further reduce the chance of attracting insects. On the other hand, organic farmers don't use any such products on the seeds before sowing them, or in the irrigation water. Actually, the average organic farmer won't use public water because that contains chlorine which is added to kill bacteria. Instead, he relies on mother nature to provide rain, which he can gather and store to be later used when there's a drought.

Once the seeds start sprouting so do the weeds and they have to be dealt with. In conventional farming, weeds are killed by using strong herbicides. In organic farming, no type of weed killer is used. The farmer will simply pull out the weeds by hand. As you can imagine, this is a time-consuming process and it requires a lot of manual labor, but at least the edible plants won't be affected by the chemicals in your typical herbicide. In addition, depending on the plants being grown, animals can be used as natural weed killers. Of course, this won't always work because animals tend to like the vegetables and plants that we like as well.

The bottom line is that organic products won't contain any trace amounts of artificial herbicides, pesticides, or fertilizers, therefore, the plants will be much safer to consume. Furthermore, the organic plants will grow at a normal pace and will have time to develop that amazing flavor we all expect to experience. Conventionally farmed produce doesn't taste like much these days because they're forcefully grown at a rapid pace with the help of chemical fertilizers.

Reasons Why Organic is Better

The human population is experiencing a steady growth rate, so producing enough food to keep everyone healthy and happy is becoming more and more difficult. Even though industrial-scale farming enables us to distribute and consume more, this farming method might not be all that viable long-term. As we can see everywhere around us, climate change and pollution are a serious problem, and farming is contributing to both. No matter the diet, we need to come up with a plan that goes beyond short-term profits and dividends. Organic farming might hold the answer, however, instead of pondering about the future of humanity, let's see what other reasons we might have to switch to natural farming methods:

1. Nutrition: Organic foods are typically richer in vitamins and minerals because they aren't forcefully grown beyond their natural ability. With enough time to develop, plants can provide us with more nutrients and more taste because we don't pump them full of chemical fertilizers that are designed to

grow the plant fast enough to gain multiple yields throughout the year. By maintaining the soil at a healthy, balanced level, we can prioritize the quality of the nutrients and taste over the quantity.

2. Supporting healthy practices: Conventional farms receive subsidies from the government for growing various products. This often leads to farmers using unhealthy and polluting practices because they're looking for pure profit. The more produce they can harvest throughout the year, the more money they receive from the government. However, that costs our health as well as the health of the environment. By supporting organic farmers, we can show investors and governments alike that organic farming is worth investing in. Thus, we can stimulate the use of good farming practices over destructive conventional methods.

3. Crop diversity: Focusing on only a few species can be risky and even dangerous. Agricultural diversity is key to healthy farming, both for us and the environment. Frequent monocultures can drain the farmland from precious nutrients, thus becoming less and less productive over the years. This is one of the reasons why intense chemical fertilizers are needed. However, monocultures aside, another related issue is planting only a

couple of select species of a certain plant. Look at the potato for instance. Nowadays, you mostly find two or three potato species at the supermarket. There's a wide variety of potatoes that we can cultivate, but we choose not to because it's easier for farmers to just specialize in one or two species. The problem here is that pests and disease evolve as well, and by farming a limited type of crop without variety, we run the risk of having that crop wiped out in the future. Organic farming seeks long-term stability and sustainability, and therefore, it's important to focus on diverse crops and species.

4. Avoiding chemicals: There's an entire chain of production that affects all of your foods when artificial fertilizers and chemical pesticides are used. For instance, conventionally farmed vegetables may contain trace amounts of those chemicals and you ingest them, however, that's not the only source of food that affects you. Farm animals are being fed with the same conventionally cultivated plants, so you might find trace amounts of the same chemicals in their meat and milk. The entire food chain can be poisoned to some degree and those toxins can transfer to you as well. One of the main reasons why organic

farming is picking up is the fact that these chemicals are transferable and can have negative impacts on our health.

Now that you have a basic idea about organic farming, let's discuss the four major principles that govern it:

1. The health principle: Organic farming has to support the health and quality of the soil and the entire ecosystem around it, including us. Its bounty feeds us without causing any significant damage.
2. The fairness principle: In this case, we're talking about having equity among all of us, and this includes all surrounding life. The food we farm is a precious, limited resource and we should use it with respect. The soil and the environment must be protected so that our future generations can take from its bounty as well. In essence, organic farming is about maintaining a high quality of life.
3. The principle of balance: We discussed earlier how conventional farming tends to disrupt the balance in nature and thus cause damage to the soil, underground water, as well as animal and plant life. Organic farming follows the principle of maintaining an ecological balance, therefore, all farming methods, whether by the book or

improvised, should work for the balance and not against it.

4. The principle of care: Farm responsibly! To benefit from farming for decades or even centuries to come, we must practice it responsibly and with respect towards our environment. The results of going against nature can be unpredictable and we can see them today in the form of severe climate change.

FROM ORGANIC FARMING TO PERMACULTURE

Organic farming is one thing, but we can take an extra step and go beyond with a permaculture garden.

Permaculture refers to having a natural system where waste is used to create a soil fertilizing cycle that can sustain itself. This way, dependence on outside interference can be lowered—even eliminated—and we can keep the soil healthy enough to produce a wide variety of produce. Permaculture can be responsible for its own waste, and therefore, the amount of pollution is significantly lowered. The main problem with fertilizers is the excess nitrogen that leaks into the nearby groundwater supply.

The main idea behind this concept is to use clever design to automate the majority of gardening chores and distribution of energy. People who dedicate themselves to the development of permaculture don't like to engage themselves in repetitive tasks. The goal is to minimize the impact on the environment and engage everyone involved in setting up and maintaining permaculture.

In essence, permaculture is supposed to mimic wild nature itself. This is what sets permaculture apart from your typical organic farming. Farming space is used in a complex manner by allowing the plants to spread the seeds themselves, and therefore, be interplanted among other species of plants. In permaculture, you won't usually see plants neatly planted in rows with barren soil around them. This system makes it easier to deal with pests naturally. Even if they aren't completely eliminated, the damage they cause is negligible.

Furthermore, energy efficiency and water conservation are crucial for permaculture to succeed. Since this farming system seeks to copy nature without man's intervention, things like rainwater, wind, sunshine, and bird droppings all contribute to the natural cycle and automated systems.

Permaculture doesn't just feed us, it also feeds the birds that, in turn, take care of certain pests and provide the soil with fertilizer in the form of their droppings.

As you can see, this form of farming combines certain organic gardening concepts with a few conventional farming practices like energy conservation and integrates everything in a self-sustaining design that has close to no negative impact on the environment.

The problem with organic farming is that even though we rely on natural fertilizer and the natural cycle of using the waste from plants as the fertilizer for others, the garden is still losing precious minerals when we take away the produce. Permaculture goes beyond in order to solve this problem. Here, food production is aimed at the local market alone. Why does this matter so much? There will always be some produce that goes bad, is unsold, or is too damaged to be used. Since the consumers are close to the production, what remains unused can go back into the permaculture cycle. Therefore, unsold produce becomes the new fertilizer, and mineral depletion takes a lot longer to occur.

However, permaculture isn't always organic or doesn't have to be 100%. This doesn't mean farmers start using chemical fertilizers. It just means that some of the plants might come from non-organic sources or at least they're not officially certified as organic.

NOURISH TO FLOURISH

Soil is essential when it comes to gardening. Without it, nothing can grow. It is not only the birthplace of various plants, but it is also their sustenance throughout their lives. Without soil, there is no gardening and in order to have your plants prosper, you need to take care of the soil on a regular basis. You could choose to buy cheap, unbranded soil, but you are running the risk of having undeveloped and even poor products in your garden. For the long-term benefits, you will have to spend both time and money to properly take care of your plants.

Since the soil is so essential, you need to take special care of it. Soil is filled with nutrients for the plants, and along with various minerals, it contains microorganisms that raise the level of nutrients in the ground. In order to work with soil, you need to know exactly what's going on with it.

TYPES OF SOIL

Almost any soil can grow something, but depending on the type of plants you want in your garden, you will have to modify the soil. There are three main types of soil: sand, clay, and loam. Each of these will be suitable for different kinds of plantlife. Gardening is not as simple as plowing the land and planting during the spring and enjoying the fruits of your labor during summer and autumn. It takes lots of effort and time to turn the soil to the right type for your planned garden. Good, healthy soil will not just feed your plants with all the needed nutrients so they grow strong, healthy, and abundant, it will also protect it from pests and various diseases.

Any soil is good enough for starting. It can easily be turned into a healthy and rich ground that will suit your needs, whether you plan to grow herbs, vegetables, flowers, or a simple lawn. All it requires is knowledge, time, and a little bit of investment. However, before you are ready to change your ground, you need to determine which type of soil you have to begin with.

1. Sandy soil will hardly keep any nutrients, no matter how much you feed it. This is because it drains easily and water together with minerals and microorganisms will simply go through it, taking it

all to the deeper levels of soil where the plant roots cannot reach. This is why, generally, sand soil is bad. However, there are some plant species that thrive and even prosper in it. Depending on what your gardening intentions are, some percentage of sand will probably be required.

2. Clay soil is very fertile as it is filled with nutrients. Plants would thrive in it if it wasn't for its texture. Clay is very hard because its tiny particles stick together. Because of this, plant roots cannot penetrate it and spread through it to soak in all the rich nutrients of clay. Clay also doesn't drain water well enough and can drown your plants. However, clay ground can easily be turned into exactly what you need in a garden. It will take some effort to turn it into proper soil, and it will need constant maintenance in order to keep it from clumping together, forming unbreachable blocks of clay.

3. Loam is an ideal soil for gardening. Like clay, it is very fertile and rich with minerals and other nutrients, but it is also crumbly so that plant roots can spread through it easily. It also drains well but keeps just enough moisture to feed the plants. This means that, with loam, you will not be at risk of overwatering and killing your plants. Loam is

something you should strive to create in your garden.

Every type of soil shares certain characteristics by which you can tell if it's healthy. Many people think that fertility is the only thing that matters and that if the ground is fertile, they can grow anything. But there is so much more to the healthy ground and all of its aspects will somehow influence your plants. Instead of relying on various store-bought fertilizers, check your soil's texture, organic matter, and pH levels.

1. Texture is nothing other than soil's 'crumb.' When you take soil in your hands and pour it through your fingers, it should fall apart and have the texture as a crumbled pie crust.
2. Organic matter. Soil needs to have plenty of dead plants and animal tissue. These will decompose and enrich the soil. Soil prepared this way is usually called humus. Humus is not just a fertile ground, it also improves the texture of the soil you already have. It will bind some of the soil particles to itself. The plant roots will enjoy it because it's easy to grow through and because the crumbs will help both drain and retain just the right amount of water. The microorganisms that live in the soil will

help break down the organic matter, turning it into the food for plants.

3. pH levels. Every soil has a certain level of acidity and this is what the pH value of your ground is. The acidity of the soil determines what type of minerals, if any, will be contained within it, and if plants would be able to absorb them. For plants such as flowers, vegetables, and herbs, you should strive for a neutral pH value, however, some plant species prefer more acidic soil. The plants you want to grow will determine what pH levels your garden should be.

HOW TO IMPROVE THE SOIL

There are some general rules you should follow if you intend to improve your soil. First things first, you need to test it and learn all that you can about the soil that is available to you. There are some tests you can do on your own, but you can also hire a specialist who can perform proper laboratory tests for you. However, this can be expensive and, usually, it is not needed and is reserved for big fields that grow food on industrial levels. For your backyard garden, you can do some basic tests on your own. They will tell you about the level of life in the ground, its pH, and its texture. These pieces of information are just enough to tell you if and what improvements to perform.

Do it Yourself Soil Tests

There is a series of simple and fast tests you can do on your own to determine your soil's texture, composition, drainage, acidity, and mineral density. The tests will also determine what kind of improvements you need to make so that your gardening ends with some great results.

The first test is called the squeeze test. It will determine what type of soil you are dealing with—clay, sand, or loam. To do it, simply take a handful of earth in your hand and squeeze it hard. For optimal results, the earth needs to be moist but not fully wet. Once you squeeze the earth, open your hand and see what it looks like. If the earth formed a shape but it crumbles easily once you disturb it lightly, that means you are the lucky one who is dealing with rich loam right from the start. However, if the earth holds its shape once you disturb it, you are working with clay. As explained before, clay soil can easily be manipulated and turned into loam. Finally, if the soil didn't even take the shape after you squeezed it and it fell apart as soon as you opened your hand, you are dealing with sand.

The second test will determine how your soil drains the weather. This is why it is named the percolation test. Generally, you want your earth to drain the extra water and remain moist enough to feed the plants. Some plant's roots can easily rot if they are soaked in too much water. This is usually what happens to some types of flowers and culinary herbs. To perform this test, you will need to dig a six-inch-wide and one-foot deep hole in the ground. Then you will fill the hole with water and let it drain completely. Fill it with water again, but this time, measure the time that it takes the ground to drain completely. Your soil has good drainage if it takes less than four hours for the earth to soak in all the water and leave the hole empty.

The third test will determine the life of your soil. To be more precise, you need to determine if there are earthworms in your garden. They are indicators of healthy soil which is rich with microbes and bacteria. To perform the test, you will need to measure the temperature of your ground. It needs to be at least 55 F and moist, but not wet. Dig a hole which is one foot wide and one foot deep. The soil you took out should be placed on a tarp or anything that will prevent the worms you possibly dug out to return to the earth. Now you need to return the earth in the whole, but slowly, sifting through it and counting the worms. For this amount of earth, you should have at least ten worms. If you have less than that, it might be an indicator of soil that lacks organic matter, or which is too acidic or too alkaline.

The fourth test is to determine the pH value of your soil. It may sound like something you should leave to lab professionals, but this is a simple chemistry test that anyone can do. Any store with gardening tools and equipment sells pH test kits. To get the correct results, you need to follow the simple instructions which come with the kit. The pH levels are labeled from 0 to 14, with zero being very acidic and fourteen being very alkaline. The plants generally love neutral pH soil, which would be somewhere around 6 and 7. If the tests show results below 5 and above 8, you are dealing with soil that will need improvement in order for plants to grow healthy.

Improving Clay Soil

Loam is considered the best gardening type of soil because it is a perfect mixture of sand, clay, mineral particles, and it also contains a heavy dosage of organic matter. If you determine that your soil is of a clay type, there are some steps you could take to improve it and turn it into loam. Unfortunately, clay soil is typical for many gardens of the United States, so people have come up with various ways to deal with it. Clay is a very fertile ground, but it is not accessible for plants. It is a very hard type of earth that will not allow the roots of plants to grow through it. Clay is also very bad when it comes to drainage and will keep too much water, which will cause the roots to rot. It also tends to be very alkaline which will influence the growth of your plants, and it is also cold and takes longer for it to warm up after winter. What you want to achieve by changing the clay type of soil is to get more drainage, perfect earth texture, and keep the nutritional values of clay. Calcium, potassium, and magnesium are abundant in clay because its negatively charged particles attract positively charged particles of these minerals.

Improving the clay soil will take effort and a little bit of time. However, once you are done, your garden will be instantly ready for planting. The maintenance you will have to perform to keep your garden healthy is easy and it will only need to be done once a year. It is easier if you improve the whole garden at once instead of making the change of the ground in each individual hole prepared for planting. Any attempt to improve the soil only around the planting hole will result in an unhappy plant with trapped roots because it won't have room to spread. Such plants may look fine, but they will stay small and won't bear any fruits or flowers. When gardening, the goal is to grow plants that will reach their full potential. Because of this, it is simply easier to improve the soil of your whole garden instead of parts of it.

Start by choosing the planting bed area and defining it. If you are using an already existing planting bed, make sure there are no plants already growing in it. If you want to keep some of the previous plants, you will have to dig them out and plant them in pots before you return them to the garden. Once you define the planting bed area, add 6 to 8 inches of organic matter to it. Ensure that the organic matter you are adding wasn't chemically treated before use. Some of the choices you have are compost (you can even make your own), grass cuttings, rotted manure, and so on. Spread the matter evenly on top of the planting area and then start mixing it with the soil. This will be done by shoveling and turning the ground so that the organic matter ends up in the soil. You will need to dig 8 to 12 inches deep. If you find digging too hard, you can also turn to till.

It will take some time for your garden bed to re-settle to what it used to be, but generally, it is already prepared for planting. During the course of time, the microorganisms in the earth will break down the organic matter, changing the texture and structure of the soil. To maintain the quality of the earth in your garden, you will have to add a new layer of organic matter once a year. The best time to do this is just before planting when you are about to dig or till the garden. If you want, you can also perform some lab testing of your soil to determine what minerals and nutrients it lacks. This will tell you what type of organic matter you will need to add next. However, wait for at least one season to pass after the improvement of the soil before doing any laboratory tests.

The typical mistake people tend to do is to add sand to their clay soil. They follow the logic of loam being a mixture of both types of earth. However, they forget that loam also has a very high percentage of organic matter in it and this is what makes it crumble. If the sand is added to the clay directly, the texture of the soil will turn into something similar to concrete. Do not do that!

Changing the pH Level of the Soil

Changing the pH of the soil usually takes some time. There are many factors that influence the pH of earth and it is enough to let the ground rest so it returns to its original pH value. However, this process is very slow and you cannot influence whether the end result will be alkaline, acidic, or neutral soil. Different plants like different pH values and you will have to plan ahead what you will plant. Because the pH value directly affects the nutrient availability, the quality of plants is directly influenced by it.

Different plants like different acidities of soil and you can manipulate it to give you the best results. For example, Rhododendrons and some berries generally like soil that is more acidic (between 5.0 and 5.5), while various vegetables and ornamental flowers like slightly acidic to neutral soil (between 5.5 and 6.5). Anything below 5 and above 7 will result in slower growth and products with less quality.

If the soil is too acidic or too alkaline, it may even kill the plant completely. High acidity attracts aluminum and manganese, making the soil toxic for the plants. But if the pH levels are showing an extremely alkaline environment, the plant can die because some of the essential minerals simply won't be available to it. Plants generally need three basic types of nutrition: primary and secondary nutrients as well as micronutrients. Primary nutrients are what plants need in large doses and they are minerals such as nitrogen (N), potassium (K) and phosphorus (P). Secondary nutrients plants need in fewer quantities, but they are equally essential as the primary. Calcium (Ca), sulfur (S), and magnesium (Mg) are considered secondary nutrients. Zinc (Zn) and manganese (Mn) are considered micronutrients and plants need them in very small amounts.

To increase the pH level of soil means to make it less acidic, and to decrease it means to make it more acidic. But before changing the pH, one must understand what influences the ground's acidity. The first factor that affects the pH is the material that the soil is made from. The base materials are rocks and rock particles. They can be either acidic or alkaline. The second factor is water or rainfall. Rain soaks the earth and continues to travel through it. However, by passing through the top layers of soil, water picks up minerals and transfers them elsewhere. The minerals will be replaced by iron and aluminum which are not good for the plants in high amounts. This means that areas with heavy rainfalls throughout the year tend to contain more acidic soil than dry places. The third factors are fertilizers used in gardening. Some tend to increase the acidity of the soil, especially if they contain urea or ammonium.

The common practice in gardening is to add the compound which contains some form of lime if you want to increase the pH of the soil. There is grind agricultural limestone available to everyone and it is the most used substance in gardening. It is important to know that if the limestone particles are very fine, they will speed up the process of decreasing the acidity. However, you need to know the type of soil you are working with in order to know which amount of limestone to add. For example, clay-rich soil will require more limestone than any soil with a lower amount of clay just to make the same pH adjustment. This is because the amount of organic matter also counts. The more organic matter, the less limestone you will need to lower the acidity of your soil.

Another useful component that can be used to increase the pH level of the soil is wood ash. It is less effective than limestone, but with frequent use, it will make the desired change. Wood ashes contain potassium, calcium, boron, and some other elements and it works well with the sandy soil. However, don't use the ashes if your plants are germinating or if the plants are very young as it could damage the vegetation in your garden. It would be best to use the ashes during the winter. Spread a thin layer on top of your planting bed, and in the spring, you can mix it in the soil while you are preparing your planting area. Don't use coal ashes because they don't contain any lime values and can even increase the acidity of your garden.

To decrease the pH value of the soil, you can choose between the two most common materials: aluminum sulfate and sulfur. Aluminum dissolves fairly quickly in the ground, and because of that, aluminum sulfate will lower the pH levels almost instantly. Sulfur, on the other hand, will take some time. With the help of the bacteria commonly found in the ground, sulfur will turn into sulfuric acid. The time it takes for sulfur to work will depend on the soil temperature, moisture, amount of bacteria in the ground, and the fineness of the compound itself. If the conditions are not optimal, it can take up to several months to decrease the pH levels of soil with this method. Most people opt to use aluminum sulfate exactly for this reason.

Both of these compounds will damage the plant's leaves if they come in contact with them. They need to be worked in the ground and it is best to prepare the soil before planting. If by any chance aluminum sulfate and sulfur come in contact with the leaves, wash them out to avoid burns. Remember that the whole garden won't necessarily have the same pH value. In order to test correctly, you will need a sample from each planting bed. Plan ahead where you want to grow certain types of plants and adjust the pH of the soil accordingly.

Soil Amendments

We already said that good, healthy soil is essential for gardening. However, gardens do not come with already prepared soil. Even if you are lucky enough to discover that your garden is mostly loam, you will need to know how to enhance every aspect of it so your fruits, vegetables, and flowers grow to their maximum potential. Soil amendments are materials that you need to add to the earth in order to change some of its characteristics. To enhance the properties of the earth, you need to know which amendments to use, and what each of them will actually do to your garden. We already mentioned aluminum sulfate and sulfur, as well as wood ash as amendments which will change the pH value of the soil. However, there are many more, and some of them you will make yourself. Plenty of materials for good, quality soil amendments can be found in nature, or even in your own kitchen.

To start improving the soil with the amendments, you need to know when is the best time to do it. Remember that healthy soil doesn't need anything, and if your plants grew well before, there is nothing to improve. However, if they didn't, there is room for improvement. The best time to do it is before planting anything, while you are preparing the ground. This is usually done in early spring but you can do it anytime you decide to start your garden.

Soil amendments can change the pH of your planting beds, the texture of the earth, and can add nutrition for the plants. The previous segment of the book explained how to test and change the pH value of the soil, while in this segment, we will concentrate on improving the texture and nutrition with organic amendments.

Compost is named the "black gold of the garden" for a reason. It doesn't necessarily contain nutrients (although it does in some quantities), but it will improve the quality of soil, change its texture, and make the minerals more accessible to the plants. Compost will also attract soil life such as earthworms, microbes, and bacteria—all necessary for a healthy garden. It can also prevent some of the soil-borne plant diseases. Compost is nothing more than decomposed organic materials such as food remains, manure, garden clippings, leaves, straws, etc. Compost preparation takes time but little to no work. All you need to do is make a compost container and add any of the numbered materials in it. Don't be afraid to mix food scraps with garden shavings or straw. In time, the materials will decompose and you don't have to do anything about it, except add more of whatever you want. You will know compost is done when you can't really say what is in it, and it looks almost like the earth itself. This natural compost preparation method may take several years in order for everything to decompose. There is a faster method but it takes more work. You will need to learn how to make each layer of the compost. To have an idea of how it is done, here is a simplified guide:

1. Find a bin that is 3x3 feet.
2. The first layer needs to be made out of brown material only such as hay, straw, or dry leaves. Make this layer 3 to 6 inches tall.
3. The second layer needs to be composed of green materials such as leaves, grass clippings, and kitchen scraps. This layer needs to be 9 to 18 inches tall.

4. Dampen the pile with some water, but do not soak it.
5. Repeat layering in this manner until your bin is full. If the bin is not full, the materials won't heat up enough to quicken the decomposing.
6. Cover the bin with a tarp so it doesn't soak too much water, otherwise, all the nutrients will be washed away.
7. You will have to turn the compost every two weeks to evenly mix it.
8. The compost is done when it starts resembling the soil. You can filter the larger chunks which did not decompose fully and continue the process by adding more material to the pile.

Remember that these are guidelines only and that there are many factors that will slow or fasten the decomposition of various materials. However, there is no right or wrong method. In any case, sooner or later, you will end up having compost that is ready to use.

Manure is a good option for adjusting the soil texture. You can easily get it from any local farms or stables. Fresh manure is not good for gardening. It contains too much ammonia and will burn your plants. Besides, the stench is unbearable, especially if your garden is in close proximity to the house. Good manure should be dry, crumbly, and with no smell. Manure is best used during the fall because it will have enough time to decompose in the soil and you will avoid burning the plants with ammonia. Any farm animal can produce manure suitable for gardening. Usually, horses and cows are used, but it can also be from sheep, chickens, goats, and even rabbits. Don't use cat or dog manure as it can contain parasites that will hurt your plants. While decomposing, manure will release soil carbon which will help make nutrients available to herbs. It can also help sand soil retain moisture or improve the drainage of compact, clay soil.

Grass clippings can be used on their own as an amendment for soil. You can mix it directly with the soil and leave it over the winter to decompose slowly. However, make sure that there are no seeds in your grass clippings as you don't want to make extra work for yourself in the spring. Also, you need to take care not to use the clippings of grass which were chemically treated. Any chemicals put directly in the soil will work against you in the long run. They can kill off microbes, bacteria, and earthworms.

Coffee grinds can be used both in the compost or on their own when you want to add nitrogen to your soil. However, putting coffee grounds directly into the soil will not add nitrogen immediately. They need to decompose naturally in order to fertilize the ground. Coffee grounds will also improve the drainage of your soil as well as its texture due to being another organic matter option. Be careful though as coffee can lower the pH of soil if it's unwashed. But you won't have problems if you opt for using cooked coffee. While fresh coffee is acidic, cooked coffee is neutral. Use fresh coffee around the plants which love acidic soil, but never spread it around your whole garden. If your garden is small, you can use coffee leftovers you gather yourself. But if you decide you need larger quantities, you can ask the local coffee shop to give you the leftovers instead of throwing them away. Besides enriching the soil, coffee grounds can repel slugs and rabbits, while also protecting your plants from some fungal pathogens.

Organic fertilizers differ from chemicals because they do not destroy the soil in the long run. In fact, they will feed the plants and build the soil structure at the same time. Because organic fertilizers are filled with organic matter, they will keep the earth well aerated and optimize its draining capabilities. They are also beneficial to earthworms and insects which are good for your plants. Instead of various chemicals, organic fertilizers are made out of plant decomposed remains as well as some rock powders. These materials take time to decompose within the soil, so be aware that organic fertilizers work slowly. Instead of excessive growth of the plants, you will get constant and healthy nutrition of the soil and plants. Chemicals will make your plants grow at an explosive rate, however, the root will remain undeveloped. This can be dangerous for plants that will grow during multiple seasons as the plant, in general, is much weaker.

When it comes to any type of amendments made out of fresh plant clippings or remains, make sure you are only using the healthy plants. Watch out for the soil transmittable diseases as you do not want to infect your future garden and the plants in it.

Mulching Your Garden

Mulching is basically covering your planting beds with a material that will protect it. The layer of mulch has many benefits: it will keep the moisture trapped in the soil, it will prevent excessive earth heating, it will keep the weed away from your plant beds, and it will protect your garden from frost and drought. Because organic mulch decomposes over time, it will fertilize the ground and add to its texture as well as drainage capabilities. Organic mulch also adds to the attractive look of the garden but it needs to be changed often because it decomposes. In general, if the mulch you are using is dry enough and contains parts of wood, it will take a longer time for it to decompose. It will also give fewer nutrients to the soil.

It is important to know the origin of the mulch you plan to use. Even though it can be bought at garden centers, check the producer and how he is making them. If mulch contains some weed seeds or it was chemically treated, it can create problems in the long run. You will have extra work plucking the unwanted weeds from your garden, or your soil will be contaminated by whatever chemical ingredient used in the mulch.

Bark mulches can be used around the trees and shrubs. They can also be used in planting beds which don't need digging often. They work well around plants that are bordering walkways, such as roses or evergreen ornamentals. Bark lasts the longest of all types of organic mulches, and it can be annoying to have to remove them each time you want to plant something new. They also don't add much to the texture of the soil or its nutrition. However, bark mulch looks very attractive and will give the impression of a neat and organized garden.

Grass clippings can also be used as a mulch if you choose not to mix them into the earth or into the compost. Instead, leave them on top of the soil as the covering. They will eventually decompose and have the properties of amendments. However, grass clippings are a bit more complicated to use. They can trap the water on the surface, not allowing it to soak in the soil. They can also become slimy with a strong odor that you want away from your house. Because of this, it is best to use them in the remote parts of the garden where they will keep the weeds at bay. If you are using grass clippings from your own lawn, make sure you do not treat it with chemicals. The best place to use the grass clippings as mulch is on the open, unplanted soil.

Newspapers were used in plant transportation for a very long time. They have an amazing ability to keep the moisture trapped in the soil around the plant's root. For this reason, and some others, it is becoming more and more popular to use newspapers as a mulch. Besides keeping the moisture in, newspapers will keep weeds away from your plant beds and they will control the temperature of the soil. Many newspapers use organic ink nowadays, so there is no danger of contaminating your plants. To use them as mulch, spread the newspapers around the plants and wet them. In order to keep the sheets on the ground so that the wind doesn't blow them away, you can cover them with some other type of mulch.

Shredded leaves are said to be nature's favorite mulch. Not just that, but they are an organic matter that will mix well with the soil after it decomposes. They also attract earthworms. Although some people don't like the looks of the shredded leaves, they are perfect for woodland types of gardens where they will look natural. However, leaves will decompose quickly and the bad appearance will only be temporary. They need to be shredded because whole leaves tend to stick to each other and repel the rain from the soil.

Straw and hay decompose very slowly, so this mulch will last you the whole season. If you are bothered with it, you can easily rake it and remove it. Straw is a natural disease repellent because it will keep the lower, sensitive parts of the plant elevated away from the soil. It will attract earthworms and spiders which will, in turn, repel unwanted pests. Straw and hay will also keep the temperatures of the soil optimal for the healthy growth of your garden plants.

PEST AND DISEASE CONTROL

Your garden is a living, breathing ecosystem. It contains much more than just your plants. Besides the beneficial microorganisms and bacteria in the earth, your garden will be home to various insects, arachnids, worms, small critters, and birds. More than 90% of the life in your garden is beneficial to the plants you are growing. They work actively to dissolve the organic matter necessary for the soil, they pollinate the plants, and they eat that small percentage of garden life which is harmful to the plants. You do not want your garden to be completely sterile and without any life except plants. The right balance needs to be achieved in order for your garden to prosper.

The easy solution is chemicals. They will kill off everything that bothers your plants in a really short period of time. However, the chemicals will also kill those little helpers, the insects that are beneficial to the plants. They may even kill precious birds. In the long run, chemicals will enter the soil and make it less fertile. Your plants will also start suffering. Unfortunately, the toxic chemicals will end up on your plate eventually.

As an organic farmer, you will have to devote a little bit more time tending to your garden in order to keep it free from various pests and diseases. Your goal won't be to destroy the insects that may harm the plants but to manage and control what is happening in the garden. Because of this, it is really important that you learn the difference between the pests and beneficial life that inhabits your planting beds. Many insects feed on the parasites and pests that hurt your plants and bring them diseases. You will want to cherish the good insects and not just keep them alive, but also to make your garden a welcoming home for them.

PREVENTION

When it comes to the successful management of pests and diseases in your garden, it all starts with prevention. After all, it is better to prevent a disaster from happening than to have to deal with it when it's too late. You need to work together with your garden in order to minimize the problems various pathogens could cause. There is no need to reach for the quick solution that chemicals are, even if the urge in you is very strong. Nature knows how to take care of itself, and we humans are there only to help. Therefore, you need to learn what is going on around your garden.

The pests and diseases attack only those plants which are under some kind of stress. They might be hurt, damaged, or lack some nutrition. A strong, healthy plant has its own ways of dealing with the pathogens, and if you take good care of them, you will prevent harmful organisms from attacking them. Taking the preventive control over your garden means that you need to do everything in your power to make the plants strong, healthy, and happy. Give them all conditions necessary for the vegetables, herbs, fruit, or flowers to grow uninterrupted and reach their maximum potential.

Even in the early stages, before planting your garden, you need to think for the future and start from the basics. The first prevention of pests and diseases comes from the soil itself. It needs to be very well aerated, adding organic matter once a year to keep it fertile. There is nothing bad with organic fertilizers, and if you want, you can include them in the yearly maintenance of the soil. You also want the earth which will trap enough moisture to be able to feed your plants. Water carries the nutrients to the roots through which they are absorbed. This is why you should never allow your plants to compete for water. Keep the soil optimal for the plants you plan to grow in it. Think well because some might like the soil that drains better, while others like more moist ground. Once you plant the garden, make sure each seedling has enough room to grow and develop without needing to battle other plants for the resources. You should also develop a habit of plucking out the weeds each time you visit your garden. Weeds are specialized in stealing the nutrients from the ground, so you need to remove them to allow full access to your plants.

After each harvest season, the garden needs to be cleaned up from the debris and leftover plant material. You might think that leaving the unused parts of the plants is beneficial to the soil as it turns into organic matter, but think again. Pests, pathogens, and insects love to hide during the winter in the debris, and leftover plants. They will multiply in them, and as soon as the spring comes, they will be first to eat and damage your new garden. Don't forget that removing the debris is not enough. Many harmful organisms live in the actual soil. After you clean up the garden, turn the earth to expose the insects as well as their larvae or eggs to the cold of the approaching winter. Birds will also be attracted by the uncovered insects and will clean your soil.

Some pests and pathogens only attack one plant species and its relatives. Because pests and pathogens live on the earth, you don't want to plant the same vegetable, herb, or flower in the same spot year after year. That is the way to provide the pests with a constant food source. You need to rotate your crops and plant different types each year. For example, broccoli and cauliflower are related plants, and it is not a good idea to plant them twice in the same spot or to rotate between the two vegetables. Plant tomatoes or cucumbers instead. Wait at least two years before planting broccoli and cauliflower on that same spot. In fact, some plants are so sensitive to the diseases that you should avoid planting them in the same spot at all costs. Potatoes and tomatoes are among those plants and it is wise to keep them rotating and planting in different parts of the garden each year.

By planting one type of crop in multiple areas of your garden, you will make it much harder for the pests to destroy all of them at once. Instead, they will concentrate on just one area. But you can even go a step further and divide the same type of crops and in between the patches, you can plant a herb which is a good pest repellent. You must be careful though and learn which crops can coexist without competition. You don't want them fighting over the resources. For example, it is not a good idea to plant tomatoes next to strawberries. Tomatoes are tall and will keep the strawberries in shade, away from the much-needed sunlight. Later, we will talk more about companion planting and what to never mix in your garden.

If you notice a plant that was attacked by a certain type of disease, you will want to remove it and destroy it before it spreads the pathogen to other crops. However, that might not be enough. People are very efficient spreaders of plant diseases. You may not be aware of it, but the pathogen might cling to your boots, hands, or even clothes, and you will transmit it to the healthy plants if you approach them directly after handling the diseased one. To avoid this, be sanitary at all times. Regularly wash the clothes you wear while working in your garden, including your shoes. Wash your hands and face before and after working in the garden so you minimize the risks of spreading the infection. You also need to take good care of your gardening tools and clean them after each use. You might even want to disinfect them and get rid of all the possible pathogens on them. A 10% bleach solution will do the trick.

DISEASE MANAGEMENT STRATEGIES

The disease is transferred to plants by various fungi, viruses, bacteria, and mycoplasma. They create lesions, burns, leaf spots, or rust on the plants. Diseases can either stunt your plants or completely kill them. They can affect one plant, a portion of your plant bed, or the whole garden. You need to get rid of the diseased plant as soon as you notice it if you want to prevent it from spreading to other crops. The best way to fight off plant diseases is to simply prevent them. The same rule applies to humans—if we keep our bodies healthy and strong, we will easily fight off any viruses and bacteria that try to attack us. Plants also have natural ways of fighting off diseases, but you have to keep them in the best possible shape so they can defend themselves.

When you buy seeds, the label will tell you the diseases that the plant is resistant to. Be aware that this doesn't mean it won't contract it, but instead, it will easily fight it off and survive. To prevent disaster from happening, choose disease-resistant plant varieties. If you are not buying seeds but plantings, you need to inspect them well. Take them out of their container and look at the leaves, stem, and especially roots. Leaves should have no spots, the stem should be firm, and the roots should be pale for young plants. Make sure there are no signs of rot on any of the plant parts.

Many plant diseases thrive in wet soil. Because of this, you want to make sure that your plant beds have enough drainage. The ground should be moist, not wet. Excessive water promotes root rot, especially in vegetables. To promote the aeration of the soil, use raised planting beds. This will keep the earth safe for your plants as the air dries the soil and kills off any harmful pathogens that might be living in the earth. You should also avoid planting in spots with deep shade as the lack of sun will keep the ground constantly wet. The soil around the house or around tall trees is perfect for the development of pathogens because the shade keeps it wet.

You should also mulch your garden. Organic mulch such as straw, wood, or newspaper will prevent the lower parts of the plant touching the ground and transmitting the pathogens to the leaves and stem. This is very important as many diseases start when the raindrops splash the earth on the lowest leaves. Not all pathogens will attack the root, and they will wait for the opportunity to find themselves on the stem and leaves of the plant. In order to secure the prevention of transmission of pathogens, your mulch will need to be at least 4 inches thick. However, the mulch will also keep the temperature of the ground lower. Because of this, mulch the warm-loving plants such as tomatoes and paprikas, only after the sun has had enough time to warm the earth.

One of the best mulch materials is plastic, and yes, even organic farmers can use it if they dispose of it properly. After the use, never leave the plastic in the ground because it takes thousands of years to dissolve, and it is not an organic matter, so it will bring no benefits to the soil. However, plastic is good for isolation and insulation. It will protect the plants coming in contact with the earth, but it will also regulate the temperature of the ground. Plastic comes in various colors, but early spring planters prefer black because it attracts the heat, warming the ground. If you plant in the late summer and you choose plants that love the cooler ground, you can use white plastic. Some of the plastic mulches even have infrared transmitting abilities allowing certain light waves to pass the barrier and benefit the soil.

Some of the plant diseases are seed born. Organic farmers like to collect their own seeds and use them in the next planting season. This practice is completely fine as long as you make sure you are not collecting seeds from the plants that were previously infected. Even if the plant survived the disease, its seed could be the carrier and you could infect the next generation.

Always check the OMRI list for approved organic fungicides and pesticides, as well as other materials used in organic gardening. They are an organization that reviews, approves, or disapproves of materials used in organic gardening, hence the name 'The Organic Materials Review Institute' (OMRI). Some gardeners use baking soda (sodium bicarbonate) or fungicide products that contain high levels of it. If you choose to do so, you need to be aware that it will kill the harmful fungi, but it can also raise the levels of sodium in the soil which may be toxic to certain plants. Other organic fungicides may include copper or hydrogen peroxide which, again, should not reach the critical levels in the soil. Powdery mildew spores are usually killed with neem oil when it comes to organic gardens because it is organic and has no unwanted effects on a variety of plants.

We already explained that wet and excessively moist areas are good breeding grounds for most of the plant diseases. To prevent this, many organic gardeners opt for high tunnels or hoop houses that use the drip irrigation system. This system will keep excess moisture from the ground as well as from the air, making it impossible for pathogens to multiply and survive. High tunnels are plastic-covered green gardens, and most people use them to prolong the growing season because they insulate the plants very well. However, the tunnels will also protect your crops from diseases and pests by keeping them isolated.

You might want to choose grafted vegetables over the heirloom ones. These vegetables have much higher disease resistance and shelf life. However, if your garden is small and you want to keep it as natural as possible, by all means, go with the heirloom vegetables. If you are a commercial gardener, grafted vegetables such as tomatoes, chilies, cucumbers, melons, and squashes are more vigorous and even resistant to pests such as nematodes. Grafting is when one vegetable is combined with another which has a completely different genetic background. The plant that has the crops you want to harvest will be grafted on a suitable rootstock. That rootstock will have the genes that will protect the otherwise vulnerable crop (scion).

The Importance of Crop Rotation

The crop rotation is an age-old method of preventing pests and pathogens from creating damage to your garden. However, it needs to be done properly in order to get the most out of it. It can be also used as a method of keeping the soil fertile. If you just switch the place of certain crops randomly, you might do more harm to the plant than good. This is because some plants are classified as heavy feeders and they will get all the nutrients out of the soil, so whatever you plant next in their spot will not have enough food. It is true that if you prepare the planting bed with organic fertilizers and compost, you will replenish the soil with nutrients, but the problem of pests and disease stays. Crop rotation is done so it provides the protection of the plants as well as the proper nutrition.

As a pest and disease control, the goal of crop rotation is to keep the number of pathogens low. By planting the same vegetable, or even the same family of vegetables on the same spot, you are allowing pests and pathogens to multiply over the years. Eventually, their numbers will be so great that the plant won't be able to use its natural defenses as it will be overwhelmed. Remember that some plants, even though they look completely different, come from the same family and share the vulnerability to certain diseases. It is easy to guess that broccoli and cauliflower share the same family—the Brassicaceae. However, did you know that cabbage, turnips, and mustard plants belong to the same family? They also share diseases such as black rot, blackleg, clubroot, and Fusarium yellows. Planting broccoli in the spot where cabbage used to be will not rid you of the problem but may even cause more.

There are some pests that have a really wide range of host plants and it can get very difficult to find a suitable crop to replace the previous one in the same spot. One such is a fungus *Rhizoctonia solani.* Besides attacking a wide range of plant families and groups, it is also resilient to different climates and can be found all over the world. It causes multiple plant diseases: collar rot, root rot, wire stem, damping off, etc. There are some varieties of crops that have a degree of resistance to these fungi, but there is no such plant that remains unaffected by it. Even the crops that have designated resistance will produce limited yield. For persistent pathogens like *Rhizoctonia solani*, it is extremely hard to find a good rotation but it isn't impossible. Some berries planted where the vegetable used to be will give decent results and the fungi won't be able to multiply.

On the other hand, there are some pathogens that can survive in the soil for many, many years. Then, the same crop family can be re-planted in the same spot after 5 to 10 years. White rot of Alliums can survive in the ground for over 50 years, and if your plants contract it, you will never be able to plant onions, garlic, or leeks in the same spot. However, this disease is specific to Alliums and you can always choose to plant another crop family in its place. Most pathogens with long soil life have a small variety of hosts and are easier to manage.

The crop rotation also affects the soil of your garden, and it is important to keep in mind more factors than just plant pests and diseases. Some plants use a lot of nutrients from the soil, while others don't. Some even add nutrients to the soil, so rotating crops each season is beneficial to your garden. It can be as simple as rotating between heavy feeders such as tomatoes, corn, cabbage, eggplant, lettuce, beets, broccoli, etc., and light feeders such as potatoes, radishes, onions, peppers, turnips, sweet potatoes, etc. Peas, beans, and cover crops such as clovers are soil builders as they release nutrients.

Keep in mind that for the proper crop rotation, you need to have more than one planting bed. It would be best if each crop had its own bed. That way, the crop rotation would have the best effect on the soil. You need to swap the planting bed with heavy feeders with light feeders the next year. For the third year, you will want to rotate again, but this time, plant the soil builders in that same bed.

Another easy to remember crop rotation is by harvest groups. You should be rotating fruiting crops with roots and then with leafy crops. However, keep in mind that this tactic of crop rotation is not perfect and exact. For example, both peppers and tomatoes are fruiting crops, but while tomatoes are heavy feeders, paprikas are light. Crop rotation by harvest group is an easy way to remember what you should be doing. It is not an exact science, but it is helpful.

Remember that all fruiting crops are summer harvested. Tomatoes, eggplants, peppers, squash, and melons are done with the harvest by the end of the summer. You can replant the beds with winter cover crops such as fava beans or winter rye. This will also count as crop rotation because you are swapping heavy feeders with light ones. To keep the rotation going, in spring, you will plant leafy crops instead of cover crops. This is how a proper crop rotation by harvest groups should look:

1. Fruiting crops
2. cover crops
3. leafy crops
4. root crops.

One of the most traditional methods of crop rotation is by the crop family. Simply put, this means that you don't plant anything that shares the family for a couple of years—usually three to five. This is because the same family plants are very similar in the usage of soil nutrients. On top of that, they are vulnerable to the same soil transferred diseases. It sounds like the smartest crop rotation because, with it, you tend to the soil and the needs of your plants, but it is very difficult to do this in small gardens. For crop rotation based on the plant family, you need more than two or three planting beds. It is a perfect solution for those farmers who produce food for the whole community, with lots of arable lands.

Crop rotation by family groups will take some serious planning because if plants belong to different families, that doesn't necessarily mean their nutrient needs are different. Plants can come from different groups but still be heavy feeders. If you swap a heavy feeder with another heavy feeder plant from a different family, the crop rotation won't achieve much. Here are some notable family groups:

1. Tomato family: tomatoes, peppers, and eggplants are mostly heavy feeders.
2. Squash family: squash, zucchini, melon, and cucumber are all heavy feeders.
3. Cabbage family: broccoli, cauliflower, cabbage, and kale are all heavy feeders.
4. Lettuce family: sunchokes, artichokes, and endives are all heavy feeders.
5. Bean family: beans, soybeans, chickpeas, and lentils are soil enrichers.
6. Carrot family: cilantro, parsley, and celery are mostly light feeders.
7. Spinach family: Swiss chard, beets, and spinach are light to medium feeders.
8. Onion family: onion, garlic, and leek are light feeders.

When planning the crop rotation by family group, first plant the heavy feeders such as the plants from the squash family. The next year, plant light feeders such as the carrot family.

In the third year, you can plant bean family plants that will replenish the soil. Fourth-year plants have other heavy feeders, but this time from a different family, let's say tomatoes. In the fifth year, you will either plant the onion family, which are light feeders, or you could spread manure over the soil and let it rest for the season to replenish the nutrients.

Companion Planting

Companion planting is a gardening tactic to ensure that the plants reach their maximum potential. Sometimes, we make unwise choices and end up with companions who bring out the worst in us. In that case, we become sad, anxious, stressed, and we do not perform at our best. It could be said that plants experience the same. One low growing vegetable will not reach its potential if it's planted in the shade of a tall vegetable which will keep stealing all the sunlight. As gardeners, we must make sure our plants are paired well, planted next to companions that will help them grow strong and healthy. This will only result in the fruitful harvest and bigger yields. Simply put, some types of plants like other types more or less. It is on us to learn which plants can be paired to the mutual benefits. Don't worry, you won't have to experiment with what to plant next to your carrots on your own. Science already has it all figured out, and all you need to do is learn.

There are many reasons why you should opt for companion

planting, no matter how big or small your garden is. Besides pest and disease control, you can control the levels of nitrogen in the soil, you can control shade for the plants that love it, and you can plan for the leverage for the plants that need it. For example, tall, sun-loving plants such as tomatoes can offer shade to spinach, a low growth, shade-loving vegetable. Or you can plant dill, a natural insect repellent next to the cucumbers which attract insects. This way, the dill will offer protection and your cucumbers will grow unbothered by the pests.

Although it sounds very simple, companion planting demands good planning. If you are planting insect repellents, remember that not all insects are bad and you will probably want to keep around 95% of them around your garden in order to fight other pests or to pollinate the plants. Here is an example of how to combine the plants in your garden in order to enjoy the benefits of companion planting:

Planting corn, beans, and squash together is an age-old method of companion planting known to the native Americans. Corn will give the support to the beans, which will, in turn, fixate nitrogen in the soil by pulling it from the air. The nitrogen is beneficial to all three plants. In return, the squash grows large leaves which shade the soil, keeping it cool and moist for beans and corn. Raccoons hate stepping on the prickly squash leaves because their feet are very sensitive, and thus, the pests are repelled.

Here are a few examples of good vegetable pairing in order to repel insects:

1. Onions will repel almost all insects and you can plant them next to any other vegetable, as long as they share the nutrient and moisture needs.
2. Radishes deter cucumber beetles, so these two vegetables should be combined.
3. Leaf miners are attracted to radishes and will chew on their leaves, but this does not harm the root, which we need. In turn, if spinach is planted next to the radishes, it will be free of pests and the leaves (part of spinach we do need) will be healthy and strong.
4. Leeks will repel carrot flies.
5. If planted next to cabbage, tomatoes will repel the caterpillars which love to eat cabbage leaves.
6. Plant horseradish next to potatoes in order to repel potato beetles.
7. Lavender is an amazing repellant of mice, ticks, and moths, and it can be planted nearly everywhere in your garden, as long as the ground is well-drained. It can also serve you as a condiment or a tea.
8. Just like lavender, mint is a great condiment and

tea, but it will also repel ants, aphids, cabbage moths, fleas, and mice. Plants like these will do well on the edges of the garden.

Flowers can be used as companion plants to the vegetables. They will attract insects with their powerful smell and keep them away from harming your crops. Besides, flowers will look lovely in your garden and will add some color and liveliness to it. Some flowers have a scent that even repels the insects, and because of this, they make amazing companions to cucumbers, cabbages, and carrots. One such flower is Marigold, and farmers rightfully call it the Queen of the garden.

INSECT MANAGEMENT STRATEGIES

Although companion planting is a great method of managing harmful insects in your garden, you shouldn't solely rely on it. There are other ways of insect management strategies that are equally effective. The longer we practice agriculture, the more we learn about the soil, plants, and insects. New methods of insect management come out every day as we experiment over time in our gardens. They tend to be even more efficient than old methods, as they came out of the need for faster and more reliable insect repelling.

It is a myth that organic farmers don't use pesticides. Consumers tend to buy organic products because they believe they will avoid pesticides. Sorry to burst your bubble, but organic farmers use more pesticides and fungicides than non-organic. This is simply because they don't use the synthetic chemicals of the typical commercial pesticide mixtures. Instead, they use organic mixtures, which are still filled with chemicals, but the source is all-natural. These natural pesticides have reduced efficiency, and because of that, farmers need to use them more often. Does the fact that they are natural make them safer for use? Not at all! Chemicals are chemicals and they are equally toxic no matter what their source is. People tend to believe that if something comes directly from nature, it must be automatically better for us and for the environment. However, nature is filled with poisons and toxins that can seriously harm us. Nature is ruthless and not at all safe. Further laboratory testing proved that organic pesticides are not much better than conventional ones.

Take the example of organic pesticides known as Rotenone.

It is a chemical derived from some sub-tropical plants which successfully killed most of the insects and pests in the garden. It was in continuous use until 2005 when the detailed testing proved that it causes symptoms similar to Parkinson's disease in rats. This is because Rotenone contains a toxin that attacks the cell's mitochondria. Thankfully, Rotenone was recognized as a hazardous substance and was pulled out from production as a pesticide (although it is still used in water as a piscicide, that's another story). The belief that natural is better just because of its source can be very dangerous.

If organic pesticides are that dangerous, how can you, an organic gardener, protect your plants? There are only two choices. You can either opt for no pesticides at all and use traps and handpicking, or you can make your own, natural, and less harmful pesticides which will repel the insects instead of killing them.

Homemade Organic Pesticides

Remember that you are a gardener, not a farmer. Your garden is smaller, and because of that, you can devote more time to it and tend to your plants with proper care. Large scale farmers simply have no time to give equal attention to each plant, therefore, they have to use pesticides and other not so safe methods of dealing with insects. You, on the other hand, can inspect each crop in detail, detect the emerging problem in time, and fight it in a way that won't be harmful to you, the environment, or the plant.

If you choose to make your own organic pesticides, you will not only be protecting your plants, you will also be aware of all the ingredients you are putting in, thus protecting you and your family. Remember that homemade organic pesticides most likely won't kill the insect, but they will repel them. This will also ensure that the beneficial insects are not harmed. Even if your homemade pesticide deters them from your garden, once the substance wears off from the plants, the beneficial insects will come back.

One of the simplest pest deterrents is pretty easy to make. All you need is baking soda, water, and a bar of mild, natural dish soap. Beware, industrial soaps are very strong and can cause burns on the leaves of your plants. To avoid this from happening, use natural dish soap which doesn't contain phosphates. All you need to do is mix all the ingredients together in a spray bottle and use them on your plants. The mixture will repel insects, but there is nothing in it that can be toxic to you and your family, not even your pets. If you choose phosphate-free soap, you will also make sure that the chemicals and toxins don't contaminate the soil if you accidentally spill the mixture. The proper ratio of ingredients is one teaspoon of baking soda and soap per liter of water. This mixture is good at repelling any type of insect from the Aphididae family.

Another spray insect repellent that uses a soap is baby shampoo spray. It is even simpler to make as the ingredients are only baby shampoo and water. The ratio should be one spoon of shampoo per 3 liters of water. This repellent is extremely mild as baby shampoo contains nothing harmful in it. It will repel insects such as whiteflies, scale, and spider mites, unfortunately not for long.

You can combine the soapy repellents with essential oils for even more efficiency. Some essential oils are amazing insect repellents because of their strong scents. You can even mix up to three different essential oils. If you use more than three, the scent will change so much that it won't bother the pests anymore. Here is an example of mixing essential oils that will repel different types of insects: add one teaspoon of basil, clove, lemongrass, or lavender essential oil for repelling mosquitoes. Add another teaspoon of cedarwood, tea tree, or pine essential oil to repel plant lice. Third, add a teaspoon of melaleuca essential oil as it repels various fungi. Lavender and orange essential oils are also great for attracting pollinating insects such as bees and butterflies, while cinnamon can help you fight off weeds in your garden.

For more ideas, here is a short list of essential oils and the insects they will repel:

1. Ants and plant lice will be repelled by peppermint or spearmint
2. Aphids are deterred by cedarwood, peppermint, and spearmint
3. Beetles don't like peppermint and thyme
4. Caterpillars are repelled by spearmint and peppermint
5. Fleas will run away from peppermint, lemongrass, spearmint, and lavender
6. Flies hate peppermint, lavender, rosemary, and sage
7. Lice can't stand cedarwood, peppermint, and spearmint
8. Slugs are deterred easily by cedarwood
9. Ticks won't inhabit gardens that smell of lavender, lemongrass, sage, or thyme

Any insect repellent mixture that uses soap should never be used on plants that are directly exposed to the sun or on leaves that have tiny hairs. If the plant has waxy leaves, the mixture will simply slide off and won't achieve any effect. Soap mixtures also need to be rinsed from the plants after three to four hours. Gently sprinkle pure water by using your garden hose and thoroughly wet the crops to make sure there are no soap leftovers. If you have no other choice and need to use it on plants that love the sun, spray it during the night and make sure you rinse the plants before the sun is out.

Garlic has a strong scent which most insects simply hate. They won't feed on plants that smell like garlic, and therefore, you can make all-natural garlic spray. It is very simple, just add 10-15 cloves of garlic and one-quarter of water to your blender. The mixture needs 24 hours to set after blending. Once it's set, use a cheesecloth to strain the chunks of garlic from the water. Then add one cup of any cooking oil. Keep the mixture tightly sealed in a glass jar for two to three weeks before using it. Remember that this mixture is concentrated and will need diluting in water once it is ready. To use it, simply mix ½ a cup of the mixture with one gallon of water. To make it even more potent, you may add one teaspoon of cayenne pepper but then you have to let it sit for 24 more hours and strain it again through a cheesecloth. Another great addition to this homemade pest repellent is mint leaves. Crush them in a blender together with garlic cloves.

There are many similar recipes for homemade organic insect repellants out there. Just make sure you choose ones that are safe not only for human consumption but for the soil too. After all, you will repeatedly plant crops in your garden, and for that, you will need healthy uncontaminated soil. Most of these mixtures will contain one or the other type of soap and oil. Be careful with these as the chemicals used in soap products may damage your plants, especially the sensitive ones. Once you make your favorite handmade insect repellant, a good idea would be to test it on a single leaf. This way, you can easily remove it if it is damaged by the mixture, and you won't have to deal with the whole garden being destroyed. Remember to spray your garden only when there is no sun, or at least no hot sun. The best time would be early morning before the sun rises, or in the evening when the sun is already gone.

Hand-Picking and Trapping the Pests

Hand-picking the pests directly from the plants is one of the oldest and most popular methods of pest control among organic gardeners. It sounds like tedious work, but if done early during the season, it will save you much trouble. Because you are picking up various insects and bugs during the time of the year when their numbers are low, you are preventing them from multiplying in your garden. It can easily be one of the most efficient ways of insect management in an organic garden. Some insects are known to spread disease, and if you notice a plant or a leaf that is infected while handpicking the pests, you can easily get rid of those too. Sometimes, early prevention is the best and by removing the diseased leaf or a whole plant, you will prevent the disease from spreading all over your garden.

The only tools you will need for handpicking the pests are your own hands, and maybe a bucket if you plan to collect them and destroy them later. If you are disgusted by the little bugs, you may want to consider using gloves. While most often you will be picking larger pests such as bugs, caterpillars, snails, and slugs, you may want to get rid of any eggs and larvae you notice. For this, you can use a small brush to help you scrape all the eggs off the plant.

The handpicking of pests needs to be done continuously throughout the season. However, if you start early, you won't have much work later. Destroying the first generation of pests will ensure that they won't multiply beyond control. Check your garden every week and pick up the pests that inhabit all the parts of the plants. Don't forget to turn over the leaves and check their backside. That is where the insects like to lay their eggs. Also, check the soil because lots of pests emerge from it. Don't forget the flying insects, they may be hard to catch, but you should always keep an eye on them too.

When it comes to trapping the pests from your garden, know that there are many varieties of traps that you can easily buy in any garden center. Just make sure they are using the organic ingredients. Many store-bought traps involve glue or other chemicals that will attract and kill pests and these are rarely organic. They pose the threat of contaminating your plants, crops, and soil. However, you can always opt for making your own pest traps. The endeavor might even give you satisfaction once you see how efficient the homemade traps can be.

The traps are different for various pest species and some of them attract insects with specific design and color, while others use baits such as scents or food. The method of trapping will greatly depend on the place you want to use it in your garden as well as on the type of pests you want to trap. Here are some ideas for homemade traps to help you get rid of pests from your organic garden.

Flowers, as well as vegetable gardens, are most often attacked by whiteflies, thrips, aphids, and leaf miners. The most efficient way to trap these is by using sticky traps. These little pests are easily attracted by colors such as yellow, blue, and white. To make a sticky trap, you can add a layer of petroleum jelly, Vaseline, or any other non-toxic sticky ingredient to a plastic plate or a cup. Then, you can hang these around your garden, in the plant canopy level. These traps need to be removed regularly, once the sticky ingredient is contaminated.

Fruit flies are common in fruit orchards and they need to be dealt with. To do so, make a simple trap out of a closed plastic cup in which you poked holes so that flies can enter. Fill the cup halfway with apple cider vinegar which will attract fruit flies. They will quickly drown in vinegar. These traps can be hanged from your orchard trees, but you must change them regularly, once the liquid evaporates.

To battle snails and slugs, you can build pitfall traps. Simply bury a jar or a cup in the ground where you notice slime trails of slugs and snails. Fill the jar with beer or the mixture of baking yeast, sugar, and water. These ingredients attract the slimy pests which will fall into the trap and drown. Make sure to elevate the trap from the ground so that beneficial insects don't get in. You may also want a raised cover over the trap to keep the mixture from diluting in the rain.

Cutworms are larvae of some moths. To feed themselves, they cut through the stems of young plants, completely killing them. There is no trap to catch the cutworms, but there is a way of protecting your young plants. Cutworms usually emerge from the soil when it's feeding time. Protect your sapling by planting it through a cardboard roll. Toilet paper rolls are great for this. Simply put the plant in the middle and plant it together with the roll, which needs to be halfway into the ground. The other half will poke from the ground, enveloping the plant like a protection collar. This way, the cutworm won't be able to approach the stem of your plant and destroy it. As the plant is growing, the cardboard will easily decompose in the ground.

Homemade traps are an easy way of dealing with pests.

However, it is not the most effective way and it should always be combined with other methods of pest control. Feel encouraged to investigate other trap designs, there are various sources out there that can help you. Many organic gardeners like to share the information and post their ideas of organic, homemade traps online in personal blogs or YouTube videos. In time, and with increased experience, maybe you will come up with your own designs and ways of trapping and getting rid of pests.

WEED MANAGEMENT

You can't be a gardener or a farmer without having to deal with weeds. Whether you plant a vegetable garden, or you just arrange a nice lawn, you'll encounter these plants that try to take advantage of all your work.

While some weeds can even be considered beautiful or useful to have around the house, most of them are troublemakers that take sustenance away from what you planted. By learning more about the various types of weeds and how to manage them, you'll be able to determine whether you need to get rid of them or allow them to stay.

WHAT ARE WEEDS?

In a nutshell, weeds are plants that are found anywhere you don't want them. Most of them are known to be useless for your garden and usually a nuisance. They grow quickly and compete with your plants for nutrients, water, sunshine, and space. Weeds also grow fast because you usually have to deal with the native ones that have adapted perfectly to the conditions in your specific locations.

All weeds will fight your garden plants to dominate over what nature has to provide them. However, sometimes, they will give you some information about the area and the quality of the soil because certain weeds might thrive in acidic soil, or in a lot of sun, or in humid places with a lot of shade. That's why the first thing you need to learn is the types of weeds.

Types of Weeds

Weeds can be placed into three different categories depending on their characteristics:

1. **Annual weeds**: These weeds typically live for up to a year. They germinate and spread during that time and at the end of the yearly cycle, they die out, allowing the new generation to take over. In this category, we include both the summer and winter weeds. The difference between them is that the winter annual weeds, such as chickweeds, will germinate during the summer or the beginning of autumn, and during winter, they enter a dormant

state to get ready to grow and spread during the spring. On the other hand, the summer weeds will germinate during the spring, develop throughout the summer, and when the weather starts getting too cold for them, they die off.

2. **Biennial weeds**: These weeds have a two-year life cycle. They germinate during the first year and the flowers and seeds will appear during the second year. Bull thistle and the wild carrot are perfect examples of biennial weeds.

3. **Perennial weeds**: These weeds are here to stay. They come back to life every year and develop deep roots. This type of weed is the most difficult to deal with because it's such a great survivalist. Just think of dandelions.

Weeds can be further split into two categories based on the family type. We have broadleaf weeds, also known as Dicot, and narrow leaf weeds, also known as Monocot. The first family of weeds is characterized by large leaves and by having long complex root systems. The narrow-leaf weeds, on the other hand, have narrow leaves as the name suggests, and fibrous roots.

Now that you know the basics, let's discuss weed control methods and how to deal with the most common weeds.

WEED CONTROL TECHNIQUES

Before we start discussing specific weeds, you need to know which control methods you can choose from. Each one depends on the type of weed you're dealing with, as well as the kind of farming methods you prefer. Here's what you can apply:

1. Prevention: The easiest way to get rid of weeds is by not having them at all in the first place. In other words, you have to prevent their growth. Also known as cultural weed control, this method first involves the elimination of available space. The tighter your garden, the fewer space weeds have to develop. This can also include the addition of mulch to prevent the sunlight from hitting the seeds and thus preventing the growth of the weed.
2. Mechanical control: This method is all about manually pulling weeds out, or performing any other mechanical action that limits the growth of

the weed, such as mowing and hoeing. This method is labor-intensive, however, it will provide you with results and it's well worth your time. Plus, it helps you stay fit!

3. Natural control: Sometimes, instead of getting rid of all the weeds, you might want to prepare or limit a special place for them. Of course, here, we're talking about weeds we might find beautiful or useful in some way. So, you might want to control the way they spread and leave a hint of the native environment in your own garden.

4. Chemical control: Some weeds can be incredibly destructive and resilient, and as a last resort, we can opt for chemical control methods. Obviously, as organic or permaculture farmers, we want to avoid using chemicals at all costs, but certain weeds like ivy and dodder can take over and suffocate your entire garden. Use this method only when the other choice involves losing your garden altogether and if the other methods aren't enough to deal with the aggressive weeds.

Finally, it all depends on you as the gardener. Some weeds are bad for the garden, but others are good or simply harmless. Some examples of such weeds include chicory with its gorgeous blue flowers, Queen Anne's lace with its umbrella-like flowers, and the Joe-Pye weed that smells like vanilla. It's up to you to decide what needs to go and what can stay.

The Chickweed Problem

While this common plant can be used in various folk medicines, it's usually a big problem in gardens or lawns because of how challenging it is to control its growth and spread. However, it's possible.

First, you need to know that there are two types of species. One of them is perennial and it's commonly known as the mouse-ear chickweed. This form of plant grows in small patches at the ground level. The common chickweed, on the other hand, is an annual weed. Both of them are best kept under control through the mechanical method. In other words, the best approach is to pull out as much chickweed as you can from the root. Their roots don't go deep into the ground, so you can pull the whole plant out with your bare hands or by using a hoe.

Keep in mind that the mouse-ear variety is a better survival and you must remove the entire plant in order to kill it. Otherwise, it will just grow back. Furthermore, while mechanical weeding is one of the simplest solutions and quite effective, it won't get rid of all the chickweed from your garden or lawn.

In this case, you have two options. You either accept that

you're going to have some remaining chickweed in your garden and continue to keep it under control regularly through mechanical methods, or you use a herbicide. Since you're going to focus on organic farming though, you might want to avoid this option unless you really have no choice. The problem with herbicides other than obviously spraying chemicals into the soil for other plants to absorb is that most of them might also kill or affect the plants you're trying to grow. Decide carefully, and if you can't remove it completely, you might as well leave a designated spot for it because you can also use it in salads. While chickweed can be quite aggressive, it still has some uses.

Getting Rid of Poison Ivy

Poison ivy is one of the most annoying plants to deal with as a backyard gardener. It's allergenic, it causes painfully itchy rashes, blisters, and makes your skin feel as if it's on fire. It's easy to work around the yard or play with your kids, and suddenly, you run into poison ivy and the deed is done. It also spreads easily and can take over your garden, thus meaning all of your hard labor was for nothing. So, let's see how we can get rid of this gardener's bane most efficiently so that we can nurture a fruitful garden.

If you already have poison ivy in your garden, you're going to have a tough time removing it. Remember, if a certain type of weed is native to your area but you don't have it in your garden yet, you need to start taking precautions as soon as you start working the land. Prevention is the easiest and most effective solution. However, if a weed like an ivy is already thriving in your garden, you'll have to choose between organic and chemical methods of removing them. Since the purpose of this guide is to push you towards developing a healthy, organic garden, we'll first focus on the organic methods. Both of them can be effective though. The only serious downside of the organic method is that it's a bit slower.

The problem with poison ivy is that, in order to get rid of it, you need to eliminate the entire plant. Even if just a small part of the root remains in the ground, the ivy will return. So, when using the organic method, you need to first make sure that you pull out the weed from the ground with its entire root system. Sounds like a lot of work, but fortunately, you can do this after it has rained. When the ground is soft and wet, you have a much higher chance of not ripping the plant apart from its root, and thus pulling out the whole root.

When you pull out the poison ivy, make sure you're adequately prepared because you don't want your skin to come in direct contact with the plant. Wear thick gloves and clothes with long sleeves. Don't start working while wearing shorts no matter how hot it is. The poison ivy secretes oil that contains the poison and this oil can also spread to other plants when they come into contact with a part of the ivy. So, leave no part of your skin exposed because the poison can be transferred.

If all of this sounds a bit scary, especially if you're allergic to the poison ivy as well, you might want to give the chemical control method a shot. Many organic farmers break the rule here because the ivy can take over the entire garden and it can be extremely harmful to humans and animals as well. Just imagine pulling the ivy out of the ground while dressed appropriately and then as a reflex you reach for your face to wipe off your sweat. That's not going to be a pleasant experience and you have little control over such habits and reflexes. Furthermore, no matter how careful you are with your weeding process, chances are you won't be able to get rid of all the roots and the plant will come back to haunt you next year. Sure, if you enjoy weeding after a few years of forcefully removing the plant, the root will become weaker and weaker because it requires a lot of resources to regrow so often.

Another organic removal method involves the use of boiling water. This will guarantee to kill the plant and its entire root system. However, if the poison ivy is growing anywhere close to plants you want to keep and nurture, you can't use boiling water. All plants die when they come into direct contact with it. So, only use this method when the weed is growing in an isolated area. Once you kill it and it dries up, you can remove it easily or even leave it as a natural fertilizer for the soil.

If all else fails and you can't use the boiling water method, you won't have a choice but to use chemical herbicides to eliminate the ivy. Sometimes even organic farmers have to forego the natural methods in order to prepare the land for an organic farmer. However, when using herbicides, you have to keep in mind that the poison ivy is a highly resilient plant and you'll have to apply the chemical more than once. That's because you have to kill its roots, and to do that, you need to apply the chemicals enough times for them to enter the roots and not just the leaves and stem. Otherwise, the weed will heal and grow back.

Controlling Bindweed

Bindweed can be troublesome for any gardener because it takes time to get it under control. But before we start discussing methods of eliminating this type of weed, you need to know how to correctly identify it.

Bindweed is sometimes referred to as the wild morning glory because of its similar looks. The plant grows as a vine that crawls and spreads over anything it can climb, such as your fence. This aspect makes it easy to notice because you'll see the vines when they start wrapping themselves around a plant, fence, wall, tree, or anything else that goes upwards. Once the leaves fully develop, you'll notice that they look like arrow tips. Soon after, the flowers will start growing as well and they look like pink or white trumpets.

Bindweed is challenging to eliminate from your garden because it has a complex and resilient root system that spreads over a fairly wide area underground. Therefore, when you try to pull the entire plant, some of the roots will inevitably stay in the ground, and over time, the bindweed will regrow. So, whatever method of removal you choose, including this mechanical one, you'll have to apply it several times until the weed stops growing or you have it under control.

Alternatives to the mechanical control method include the use of herbicides or boiling water. Either method will kill the plant completely if you can apply them correctly. However, ideally, you want to use boiling water and herbicides only where you don't have any useful plants you want to keep. So, if you find bindweed growing all over your fence or through the cracks of your driveway, you can safely pour boiling water or use herbicides if you're fine with it.

To use the boiling water method correctly though, you need to make sure you pour the water up 8-10 centimeters away from the stem of the plant. This is the only way to make sure you'll kill off the entire root system or at least enough of it to weaken the plant so much that it dies. If you choose to use a herbicide, you'll have to reapply it multiple times whenever the plants start regrowing.

However, there is an alternative to all this. Simply cut the plant at the ground level whenever it grows. By doing this on a regular basis, the plant will grow weak over time by using all of its resources to grow back. With each cut, you'll have a weaker, more sensitive bindweed that you can eventually kill by repeatedly cutting it.

Finally, if all else fails, you can examine the problem from a different angle. Bindweed often grows where the quality of the soil is poor and not many other plants grow there. Bindweed likes open space and if your plants or your lawn don't grow compact enough, the weed will take over. If this is the case, you can use organic fertilizers to improve the quality of the land and plant as many plants as possible. The more compact you can grow them, the more they will compete with the bindweed for the resources. By having a compact growth, however, the weed won't be able to dominate.

Controlling White Clover

White clover is a weed that some gardeners love and others hate. It really depends on whether you want to get rid of this plant or simply control it instead. Eliminating the white clover altogether can be difficult, but it is possible if you have enough determination. But first, let's learn how to identify this weed.

The white clover is a perennial plant that grows close to the ground. It usually prefers to grow on lawns where the grass doesn't grow compact enough to fight it off. The plant is easy to recognize, however, because it's clover and it grows sets of three small leaves in the shape of a teardrop. The flowers are white and elongated with a green or brown center. The plant spreads in a crawling manner, taking any available space. In fact, it's not that picky when it comes to growth areas. They basically grow wherever there's some open space left for them due to sparse grass and other plants.

With that being said, the easiest way to get rid of most of the white clovers in your yard is by growing a healthy lawn. The best solution is to improve the quality of the soil in such a way to provide nutrition for all of your desirable plants. White clover isn't the best competitive weed around, so other plants can easily fight it off until it stops growing. Furthermore, this weed likes soil that is low in nitrogen, so by fertilizing it, you'll already reduce the chance of it growing. Another control method involves the use of mulch which can be dispersed around your flowers, for example.

Having a layer of mulch will prevent the white clover seeds from sprouting.

If your yard or garden is already filled with white clover, you can remove it with any of the mechanical methods without too much effort. The plant is fairly easy to pull out with the root included, especially after a bit of rain. The only problem here is dealing with the clover seeds. They are made to survive whether it's hot or cold. They can even preserve themselves in the ground for several years before germinating, so they can always surprise you. Every year, you'll have to pull out new plants and gradually get their population under control through regular yard work and maintenance.

Finally, you can use herbicides as well but only as a last resort if the plants drive you crazy. The problem here isn't just the introduction of chemicals to your organic garden or yard. It's the fact that the only herbicides that can kill this weed effectively are those that are non-selective. In other words, a herbicide that kills white clovers will also kill any other plants it comes into contact with. So, try to avoid using this method at all costs. The white clover can be a pretty plant and it doesn't do any serious damage. You can easily keep it under control by allowing your own plants to grow more aggressively and dominate over the designated space, and by removing the weeds mechanically.

CHOOSING YOUR CROP

So far, we've discussed everything from managing soil to pest and weed control. You now know the basics of what it takes to start growing and maintaining a backyard garden or even a farm. But what about the crops? How do you choose what to plant? How do you pick your seeds? When is it time to harvest everything?

All of these are questions you should be asking yourself when starting out, and in this chapter, we'll explore these aspects until you have all the right answers.

CHOOSING SEEDS

Many people choose to buy organic seeds, but they don't really know why. They automatically assume organic means they're better and healthier. But what's the real reason for choosing them over conventional seeds or heirloom seeds?

As already mentioned, organic seeds are seeds that come from organic plants that result from only using organic gardening or farming techniques. This is the only way to have foods or seeds certified as organically produced. Many people think that organic seeds are those that have had no exposure to any kind of chemicals while growing on the farm. This isn't exactly true. After all, organic farmers use organic chemicals and some of them can be more harmful than synthetic ones. Remember, pretty much everything contains some chemicals.

Natural doesn't automatically translate to healthy. Organic chemicals are often used in higher quantities due to the lower effectiveness, for example. Therefore, organic seeds can't be completely free from all chemicals, unless maybe you planted your crops somewhere deep in the woods in the middle of nowhere and you left them alone to grow like wild plants (highly unlikely). In fact, seeds from wild sources don't officially count as organic seeds because they aren't sourced from a certified organic farm. This creates another problem because the organic seeds we're forced to use come from a very limited gene pool. This fact alone is the opposite of organic conventions. So, as you can see, there's already a difference between organically certified and truly organic in principle.

Furthermore, you also have heirloom seeds to choose from because they can be organic as well. In the field of farming (pun intended!) heirloom refers to the seed's genes that translate to stability, genetic variety, and field pollination.

So, why should you get organic seeds instead of conventional ones?

One of the best reasons to get organic seeds over any other is that they're going to sprout plants that are already adapted to the organic farming environment and techniques. Even if conventional seeds seem fine to you, if you plan to use nothing but organic gardening methods, they won't do so well. Those seeds are adapted to work well with various types of fertilizers, pesticides, and herbicides. When you don't use any of those, the seeds won't perform as well as their organic counterparts. Furthermore, by not using strong chemicals to protect your plants from weeds and pesticides, you're going to need a variety of seeds that are already naturally resilient against such problems.

Organic seeds are harvested differently from conventional seeds to make sure they're ready to survive in an organic garden. The farmer will leave a percentage of his crops to fully ripen until the seeds are fully matured. These plants will be well taken care of until the end of their lifecycle and only their seeds are going to be harvested. This way, the best viable seeds are guaranteed to end up in your hands, ready to start planting. This thorough selection process ensures that you receive the seed from the toughest and most resilient plants that have the strongest genes.

On the other hand, while conventional seeds are left to mature for just as long, they don't follow the organic principles. This is mainly due to laws and regulations. Seeds don't fall into the food category, so farmers can use any herbicides and pesticides they want in order to make sure the seed plants ripen. If you plan to become an organic farmer, you need to get your seeds from reputable sources—from farmers that care about the environment and do everything in their power to maintain a healthy balance that promotes a good life for everyone.

CHOOSING YOUR VEGETABLES

When you start making plans for your garden, it's easy to get excited but it can also cause confusion and frustration. After all, there are so many vegetables to choose from. And then each one of them comes in different varieties! Deciding what to plant in your garden is fun, but it can be difficult and you might go overboard and grow a lot more than you need.

You should begin your planning by first thinking about the purpose of your garden. Is your goal to fully replace the produce you buy from the store with your own? Do you want to just supplement your diet with freshly grown vegetables? Do you want to eat purely organic and save some money at the same time? Do you want to pickle and preserve various vegetables? Do you want to make a small business on the side through gardening? Depending on your answers, you'll have the general idea regarding your garden and that's when you can start thinking about what vegetables and herbs to plant. The more you manage to narrow down your goals, the easier it will be to choose your vegetables.

With that in mind, here's a number of things you can consider after you figured out your goals:

1. **Plant only what you like to eat**. If you don't plan to focus on what sells well, then you should grow only what you like to eat regularly. There's no point in investing a lot of time and energy into

growing something you and your family aren't fond of. If you really love salads, focus on greens, lettuce, tomatoes, and onions. Just think of what you buy from the store and make it your goal to cultivate that.

2. **Choose vegetables that like your climate**. You'll have a much easier time if you grow vegetables that like your soil and weather. You can try plants that have completely different requirements, but then you'll need to manage them a lot more, otherwise, they can die due to too much rain, sandy soil, cold nights, and whatever else isn't suitable for certain plants. The easiest way to figure out what to plant is by just looking around other gardens in your area. Speak to your neighbors and they'll tell you what they tried and what works well. Gardeners aren't usually a competitive bunch, so listen to their experiences and challenges.

3. **Plant valuable crops**. This advice isn't necessarily aimed towards a gardener that plans to make some money on the side, even though it works just as well. This is about all those vegetables and herbs you rarely buy because of how expensive they are. Just think of lettuce, garlic, and bell peppers. They're pretty expensive, and depending on your budget, you might be waiting for a sale

before purchasing them in larger quantities. So, figure out what you like that is normally a bit pricey and plant that in your garden. Seeds are much cheaper than buying organic produce regularly. Herbs are also valuable and they usually have a much stronger flavor when taking them fresh from your garden because you can ensure their quality. You can also easily preserve them and you won't need to buy herbs ever again.

4. **Plant resilient vegetables**. Some vegetables aren't as strong as others and they require the use of pesticides to fight various diseases and pests. However, there's a number of vegetables such as peppers, potatoes, spinach, and tomatoes that don't need such help to thrive. You can easily grow them without the use of any chemicals (natural or otherwise).

5. **Focus on what's easy to grow**. If you're a complete beginner or you have a demanding job that doesn't allow much free time, you'll want to plant vegetables that don't require much attention and care. We'll focus on these vegetables in the next section to give you a rough idea about what you can grow without breaking a sweat.

6. **Grow vegetables you can preserve**. If you love pickling and preserving vegetables, then you

need to plan for that, otherwise, you won't have enough to eat fresh. Finding the right combination might take you some time if you aren't sure about you and your family's consumption. So, if you're just starting out, it's ok to start with a smaller garden and figure out over time what you need more of. You also need to take into consideration that some plants keep growing new fruit throughout the season (tomatoes), but others only grow once (carrots).

Once you decide what your goals are and what you want to grow, you need to start organizing yourself by preparing a list of everything you want to plant, plotting your garden or farm, and then buying the seeds. The better you plan, the easier time you'll have working and managing your garden. And if you're a complete beginner, you should probably start with the vegetables that are the easiest to grow.

The Easiest Vegetables to Grow

If you're completely new to gardening or farming, you're probably worried about doing a whole lot of work for nothing. Don't worry, nothing is 100% certain when it comes to gardening because of how many factors can influence the end product. However, there are a number of plants and vegetables that are ideal for beginners because of how easy they are to grow as well as their resilience. Here's a list of such plants to get you started no matter how experienced you are:

1. **Carrots**: Every single garden needs to have carrots. Fortunately, they're really easy to grow and don't require your constant attention. All you need is to prepare a plot of land for them by removing as many rocks as possible without too much heavy work. If your garden is too rocky, the result will be misshapen carrots. However, they're still good to eat because the soil only influences the shape of the root. So, if you don't care about aesthetics, just plant your carrot seeds into the designated spot and wait for their green leaf tops to grow out of the ground. From that point on, the longer you wait, the bigger the carrots, so harvest them at any point because they're ready to eat.
2. **Green beans**: Beans come in many colors, shapes, and sizes, and they're all quite easy to grow. Broad beans and bush beans are probably the easiest to manage. They don't require a lot of work and they don't have many destructive pests you'd have to deal with. In any case, they're worth the effort because you can freeze them or eat them fresh throughout the winter.

3. **Lettuce and spinach**: Whether you want leaf lettuce, head lettuce, arugula, or spinach, they're all so easy to grow that a child could do it. All you need to do is successive sowings every couple of weeks so that you can spread out your harvest. Spinach is also a must-have due to the high iron content and the fact that you can add them to many salads, soups, or egg-based breakfasts. They also grow continuously if you regularly rip a few leaves from each growth.

4. **Tomatoes**: These plants are easy to start growing, especially if you buy and plant them as starter plants instead of sowing seeds. Tomatoes are fairly easy to grow and they will enchant you with their fruit all summer. However, you need to watch out for pests and diseases affecting the leaves or tomatoes.

5. **Cucumbers**: This vegetable loves to spread itself all over the garden if you allow it. Cucumbers need space so their roots can sprawl and they also like to climb on any upward object. Consider planting them next to your fence if you don't want to set up any wiring system over which they can spread.

6. **Radishes**: They are the ideal plant for beginners because all you need to do is plant the seeds straight in the soil once spring or autumn is about to start.

Radishes don't usually require any kind of special care. Just remove any weeds you might find competing with them.

7. **Bell peppers**: Similarly to tomatoes, you should plant them as starter plants to have an easier time and manage them less.
8. **Basil**: You can't have a garden without this aromatic herb. But why basil in particular? Truthfully, you can plant a number of aromatic herbs because some of them aren't that picky when it comes to weather, but a lot of them are. Basil is very easy to grow indoors or outdoors. All they need is a bit of sun, well-drained soil, and some occasional watering. To use the herb, just pluck out the number of leaves you need and at the end of the summer, you can dry them and use them in your cooking until you have fresh basil next year.
9. **Squash**: You want this plant in your garden because it's highly productive, so you'll only need a handful of them. They're easy to grow as long as you plant them somewhere that they're safe from wind because they don't like it.

There are other plants that you can easily grow as long as you live in the right area for them, your soil is appropriate, and you don't have major pests and diseases that require serious expertise. Gardening can be intimidating at first, but you'll soon realize how much it's worth your time when you finally get to enjoy the fruits of your labor.

WHEN AND HOW TO HARVEST DIFFERENT VEGETABLES

To enjoy the most explosive flavors your vegetables can provide, you need to know when exactly to harvest them. There are many factors that influence a plant's harvesting time and there aren't any solid rules about the time when you should start picking the fruits of your labor. Flavor and taste can't be determined by the size and color of the vegetables at all times. What you can do instead is learn when you can start tasting the vegetable and when you find the flavor suitable, it's time to harvest. However, in general, most plants need to be harvested right before reaching maximum maturity. With that being said, here are some guidelines for the most common vegetables you might have in your garden:

1. Asparagus: You can start harvesting the asparagus spears when they're around seven inches long. Just make sure to snap them close to the ground level so that new ones can grow. Asparagus continues to produce throughout its season up to a month and a half since you first started harvesting. At that point, even if they continue growing new spears, you should let them develop themselves to stay healthy and survive beyond the harvesting season.

2. Beans: If you're looking for the green variety and not their seeds, you should start harvesting them before the seeds become visible under the skin. The best time is when you can snap the bean in half with a clean, crunchy motion. Start testing your beans early so that you don't end up with tough, chewy and stringy beans.

3. Beets: They can be consumed at different development stages depending on your preference. For example, you can even eat the green tops. You can also begin harvesting the root itself as soon as it breaches through the surface of the soil.

4. Broccoli: This vegetable is only good when you have closed flower buds because that's what you're essentially eating from this plant. Avoid those that have already flowered and check up on your broccoli every day when it's warm. They bloom

quite fast and it's easy to miss out on the harvesting opportunity.

5. Cabbage: To test the cabbage and see whether it's ripe or not, you should squeeze it gently. If it feels solid to the touch, then it's mature enough for consumption or for pickling. Don't let it grow too large because it can continue maturing until it starts splitting wide open.

6. Carrots: They can be a bit tricky because you can't see them. All you see is the green top and you have to judge the size of the root based on how large and wide the top is. The bigger the top, the bigger the chance of pulling out a mature carrot. When you can't be sure, just start picking one or two carrots to judge their size. You can leave them in the ground until the frost comes because that will even sweeten them a little.

7. Corn: Pay attention to the corn's silk strands. It takes around three weeks since they're formed for the corn to ripen enough for harvesting. Of course, this can depend on the type of corn you have and the climate in your area, but as a general guideline, you can start picking your corn when the silks turn brown. Furthermore, you can also press on the kernels and if they release a milky-white liquid, then the corn is ready for harvesting.

8. Cucumber: One day they're too small to eat, the next they're huge! Cucumbers are tricky because they can surprise you at any time. You should check on them daily and harvest the ripe ones because they don't all ripen at the same time. They continue growing throughout the season, so pick them daily as soon as they're firm and large enough. If you leave them alone for too long, they will taste bitter and turn yellow.
9. Eggplant: When the fruit of the plant is firm and completely dark in color, you can start picking them. You shouldn't allow them to reach full maturity because they can turn a bit bitter.
10. Garlic: You can start eating garlic when it has long, green healthy leaves. At this stage, you can dry them for preservation, but you can enjoy them green in a salad or on their own. Harvesting season is only when the leaves turn brown and fall to the ground. That's when the bulb is large enough for the picking. Dig your garlic out and store it in a dry place so that the bulb can dry out and be used throughout the year. You shouldn't try to pull them out of the ground because you might break them and you should also avoid washing them before storing them. Just brush off the dirt.
11. Leeks: You can harvest them as soon as they

measure around an inch in diameter. The best thing about leeks is that you don't have to harvest everything at once. You can even leave them in the ground throughout winter and harvest them whenever you need them.

12. Lettuce: You can start by first harvesting the outer leaves only. They're ripe when they're around four inches in length. At this point, you should leave the inner leaves alone so that they can grow into new mature leaves. If you use this harvesting method, the lettuce will continue to regrow until the season is over.

13. Onion: Use the same method you used for garlic. The harvesting season usually coincides with both of them, and the onion needs to be dug out and dried the same way.

14. Peas: Test the pods to see when they're full. However, don't let them ripen until they're fully grown and bulging out. If you harvest them right before that happens, you'll get to enjoy sweeter peas. The easiest way to make sure you get the right flavor out of them according to your taste is to try them out every few days. When you find the flavor you're looking for, harvest them all.

15. Potatoes: If you're looking to eat 'new' potatoes that haven't developed a thick skin yet, you need to

harvest them right when the potato plant starts to bloom. Form an outer perimeter that is several inches wide around the plant and start digging for the potatoes. If you want to let them grow to full size, you should wait for the plant to dry out. By the time it turns brown, the potatoes should reach full maturity.

16. Pumpkin: When the vines start withering, the pumpkins should be ripe enough. Pay attention to their color on a regular basis when they start looking large enough. They're supposed to change color when becoming ripe. As a final test, you should poke the pumpkin with your nail. If you can't break through its skin, then it's ready for harvesting.

17. Radishes: These vegetables reach maturity quite fast so you need to be on the lookout for their bulbs popping out of the ground. They should be harvested on a regular basis because they can grow too tough to eat or reach the seeding stage. Because of this, it's a good idea to plant your radishes successively and not all at once. That way, you can always have fresh, young radishes.

18. Spinach: Spinach is harvested pretty much just like leaf lettuce. You pick individual leaves and let the plant grow new ones. Continue harvesting the

mature leaves until the plant starts to fully mature. At that point, you can cut the stem to use it in its entirety. If you leave it to develop further, it will start to seed.

19. Squash: No matter what type of squash you plant, you should check it frequently and harvest on a regular basis. You want them while they're young, sweet, and tender.

20. Tomatoes: Wait for the tomatoes to be fully red, or whatever color the species you planted is supposed to be, and then check to see if they're a bit soft. Pick a tomato and pay attention to the smell of the vine and how easily it lets go of the fruit. Finally, taste the tomato to see if its flavor is to your liking and then harvest them as they ripen.

21. Turnips: You can tell a turnip is ripe when it's around two inches in diameter right above the ground. At this point, it should be harvested, otherwise, it will mature entirely and attain a wood-like texture that nobody wants.

22. Watermelon: The ripeness of the watermelon is always debatable. Some claim that the sound the melon makes when you tap it with your fingers can tell you when it's ripe. If it sounds like a hollow space, then it should be ripe. Other people say it's ripe when the spot on the side of the melon which

sits on the ground changes its color from white to yellow. Both can be true but not always accurate, so judge your melons with extra care and when you think they look ripe, try one and see.

There are many more vegetables and herbs out there for you to try and plant. These are just the most common ones typically found in any diverse garden. Nonetheless, you should probably purchase a book that focuses on hundreds of vegetables, giving you detailed information on each one. It's always good to have a few gardening encyclopedias around the house. If not, you can always give Google a try.

SAVING THE SEEDS

Saving the seeds of your own vegetables comes with a number of benefits. It's an old tradition that exists in gardening since people first started planting crops. It does involve a lot of work though, and you may be wondering why you should bother when you can just go and buy the seeds every year. Well, first of all, you're going to have to save all that money. Secondly, by harvesting the seeds from your own plants, you'll create a new generation of plants that will be even better adapted to survive in your particular soil and weather. Each generation of plants will evolve and become more productive because it's adapting to your area. Furthermore, this leads to higher yields as well and allows you to plant those particular varieties of vegetables that were so tasty.

Certain plants will produce a large number of seeds without much effort because of their higher yields. Other plants like squash varieties will also produce a lot of seeds but it's generally not recommended for you to save them. Growing exactly the same squash variety year after year is unlikely to work, and at some point, you'll end up with inedible squash that can no longer fully mature. On the other hand, we have beans and peas that produce a lot of seeds that work just as well for the next season.

Saving your own seeds isn't rocket science, but it involves going through three processes:

1. Choose only the seeds from your best plants.
2. Harvest the seeds when the plant has reached maximum maturity, not too early and not too late.

3. Store them correctly, otherwise, you'll end up with rotten, spoiled seeds.

Choosing the Seeds

If you're just starting out, you should first focus on saving seeds from tomatoes, beans, peas, and peppers. They're the easiest to harvest and they produce many seeds that don't require a lot of work to store them correctly.

Next, you have the plants that aren't self-pollinating but have male and female flowers (think of corn). These vegetables can be hybridized, and therefore, maintaining a clean variety is challenging due to cross-pollination. In time, the shape and taste of the vegetable can change, and this also includes the quality of the seeds as well. This is one of the reasons why you shouldn't bother saving squash seeds.

Finally, we have seeds that come from the biennial plants. They take two years to mature enough to produce the seed. Beets and carrots are perfect examples here. If you want to harvest their seeds, you're going to have a tough time because you'll need to keep the plants healthy for two entire years. Maintaining perfect conditions for them for so long can be quite the challenge.

Whatever you do, you should save the seeds from open-pollinated plants and not the hybrids. In other words, you want heirloom varieties that have been adapting over time, generation after generation. The vegetables you'll get from these seeds will be very close to the original parent vegetable. The only real difference is that they have adapted to thrive and survive in a specific area.

The hybrid seeds that you normally find in commercial sources are produced by combining the characteristics of two different plants. For instance, they may take a variety that has a high tolerance to diseases and combine it with one that produces high yields. These seeds are known as F1 hybrids and you can spot them by reading the label. If you planted any vegetables using these seeds, you shouldn't save their seeds because they won't result in a plant as good as the parent they came from. In fact, these seeds tend to lack fertility and will often not come with the same characteristics as the parent plant.

Harvesting the Seeds

Look for the strongest, most developed vegetables in your

garden when choosing the seed and don't harvest from the weak or sick looking ones. This gives you the best chance of having a better, more resilient crop next season. With that in mind, let's discuss the seed coming from the easiest to manage plants, namely tomato, pepper, beans, and peas:

1. Tomato seeds: Allow the selected tomatoes to fully mature and then gather the seeds together with the pulp by using a spoon or a scoop. Place everything inside a jar filled with water for several days. Every day, you should stir the contents of the jar to separate the seeds from the pulp. When the seeds are entirely separated, they should sink to the bottom of the jar. Remove the water and pulp and place the seeds on a dry paper towel for a couple of days to soak out all the moisture. Then just leave the seeds to dry in a cool, dark place.
2. Peppers: Allow the peppers to fully ripen until you see wrinkly skin. Then you can remove the seeds and place them directly on a paper towel to dry them out. Once they're dry, you can store them inside a paper envelope.
3. Beans and peas: Once the pods reach full maturity, you'll see that the pods have turned brown and they're dry. You can now remove the seeds and spread them evenly apart from each other inside a

tray. Leave them like that to dry for a couple of weeks. You can also just leave them inside the pods and dry them the same way.

To store the seeds, the cheapest and most practical solution is using paper envelopes and then placing them in a dark, dry place where moisture can't get to them. You can also use a container to seal them in from the outside environment. Don't forget to write on the envelope what they are and when you harvested them so that you have an easy time sowing them.

Finally, you can swap your seeds with other organic gardeners to share your vegetable varieties and try out new things. If you plan to try this, you should perform the swap in your own area to guarantee that the seeds you receive are already acclimated, otherwise, you might end up with a weak harvest.

GETTING YOU STARTED

Now that you have the knowledge of what it takes to be an organic gardener, it's time to get you started and equip you with even more knowledge. Organic gardening is one of the best ways to know exactly what you and your family are eating. Your organic garden will be beautiful and will attract bees, birds, butterflies, and small critters which will only bring more life and beauty to your backyard.

You can always choose to hire a professional to set the layout for your new organic garden and to start it. But where is the joy in that? People choose to start a garden because they are attracted to it, and they observe it more as an enjoyment than work. After all, starting your own organic garden is not a difficult task at all. All it takes is for you to roll up your sleeves and put in some effort. The work you will have to do while preparing your garden beds is not easy, but it will heal your body and your soul. It is no wonder many ancient philosophies teach gardening as a way of growing not just the plants, but yourself as a person.

CHOOSING THE RIGHT SPOT

When you look at your backyard, you probably wonder what could grow in it or if there is enough sun for certain types of plants. Is there shade, water, and the right kind of soil? These are questions that are common to both new gardeners and experienced ones who are starting to cultivate a new piece of land. Luckily, the answers to these questions are not a mystery and you can do some testing and determine how to improve the soil and choose the right spot for various types of plants. If you are new to gardening, you do not have to plan big and turn your whole backyard into a garden. Starting with one type of plant but doing it properly is much more satisfying. You can add more plants next season, or later during the summer and autumn.

Believe it or not, one of the most important factors when choosing a spot for a garden is convenience. This is because the garden is happier the more you attend to it. To do so, you need to have quick access to it. This will inspire you to spend half a day working in your garden. The work doesn't need to be necessarily tiresome and hard. Simple handpicking of some pests and weeds each day will keep your plants happy and thriving. In time, as your garden grows and turns your yard into a beautiful, magical place, it will attract more people to spend time there. With some help from the children or spouse, it will even become pleasant working half a day with the soil and plants.

Another important factor is sunlight. The majority of garden plants such as flowers, herbs, and vegetables enjoy the sunshine. Fruiting vegetables especially love the sun, and it would be smart to choose a place for them with at least 6 to 8 hours of sunlight. Leafy vegetables and herbs are happy with 4 to 6 hours of sunshine. Some plants like shade and don't forget to take them into account too.

In order to determine which part of your future garden is best suited for certain types of plants, you will need to measure the sunlight. However, this is not a hard task. There are three very simple ways you could do it:

1. Chart the sun. Make a chart of your yard with the divided areas for planting. Add the hours from sunrise to sunset on each planting area. Once an hour, you will go out in your yard and note which area is in full sun, part shade, or in full shade. This will give you a pretty good idea of how many hours of sunlight each of the designated planting areas has

and it will be easier for you to decide which plants to grow where.

2. Map the shade. For this, you will need three copies of the plan of your yard. You can either use a property survey or Google satellite images of your property. Finally, you can always make your own sketched map and copy it 2 times. Now you will have to observe where the shades are from 10 am, 1 pm, and 4 pm. Color the areas that are covered in shade on a separate map copy for each time period. Compare the maps to see which areas are uncolored and you will get the spot with the most sunshine.

3. Get a sun measuring tool. There are various tools specifically designed for gardeners to measure the sunlight easier. For example, SunCalc is a tool you will need to stick in the ground in the wanted planting area. Leave it there for one full day and take the readings in the morning of the following day.

Soil is another factor that will influence how you plan your garden. In chapter 2: Nourish and Flourish, we talked about the soil in great length. The fact that soil has its own chapter in this book shows you how important it is. That's because earth is the life-giver for the plants. It contains all the necessary nutrients for vegetation to grow strong and healthy. In order to get a better understanding of the soil in your garden, perform the tests described in chapter 2. You will learn what type of earth is at your disposal, its pH, drainage, and life it contains.

Remember that you can manipulate the soil and don't despair if it's too sandy or made out of clay. Make a plan of the garden with divided planting beds and perform a test in each one of them separately to see if the earth is different in different parts of your backyard. Then you will know exactly how to treat the soil to make it more fertile, drain better, or to have just the right texture.

You may want to do the laboratory tests of the garden's soil. This will give you a detailed insight into what nutrients it lacks or what it contains. The local agriculture institute will offer such tests and they don't have to be too pricey. You can choose what to test the soil for. It can be just a pH test, but the advice is to include phosphorus and potassium levels as these two elements are used by plants in large amounts. You can also test the garden's soil for micronutrients such as zinc, iron, or manganese, but if you feed the earth with compost each year, the chance of having the problems with micronutrients is very thin.

Besides the sun and the soil, plants need a third element which will determine their health and growth. It's the water. Some plants like constant moisture, others like well-drained soil. The third ones like a healthy periodical change between moist and dry ground. However, all seeds need moist ground while they are germinating. This means you will have to water your garden regularly. Water is what brings the nutrients to the plant through its roots, and without it, the plants would simply starve. Even the most resilient plants that live in desert-like conditions require at least some amount of moisture to be able to absorb nutrients.

While planning your garden, even before seeding, you need to think about the access to water and how you will bring it to your crops. You can use a hose, a watering system, a sprinkler, or carry the water to the plants in buckets. The water source is equally important. The best water for plants comes from the earth itself as it already carries various minerals and nutrients. You may choose to dig a well. Rainwater is also good for gardens and you can build rain collectors somewhere near your house to collect the water from your roof. The third option is city water, but it may not be the best choice for the garden. It can contain too much chlorine and other chemicals that can influence the soil and alter its pH values. Make sure that the water in your town is good enough for gardening. The water supplier is obliged to display what he adds to the city water and this information is available to everyone, usually with just a few clicks on the internet.

These factors will greatly influence how you plan and set up your garden. Think well and understand that you won't be doing much if you only take the sunshine into account. You need to plan by observing all the factors mentioned above. The plants need sun, soil, and water, and if any of these three are lacking somehow, the crops won't yield much if anything. As for the convenience of the garden, that is all up to you. You can also think about the decoration, paths for pets and children, resting area and so on. Gardening should be a pleasure and you should think about how to make it enjoyable for you and your family. You can even think about setting up a gazebo or garden chairs and table so your friends and family can share the beauty of your garden.

BASIC GARDENING TOOLS

Now that you have an exact plan in your head and you know all the conditions of your backyard, you can start turning it into a beautiful garden. The work can finally begin. However, for this, you will need certain tools. Beginner gardeners easily fall into a trap of buying all the unnecessary gear that a local garden center has to offer. This happens due to too much information out there which may overwhelm you. There is no need to buy literally everything simply because gardening tools are often versatile and can be used for more than one action.

The idea of this section of the book is to give you a comprehensive list of useful tools, concentrated in one place. The danger of doing your own research on tools lies in information being scattered over the internet and the written sources, and they usually contradict each other. You can come back to this chapter whenever you need to look up a new tool—if nothing else, to get the basic idea of its usefulness and necessity.

1. **Gloves** are probably the first tool you should think about buying. They are the protection for your hands, and even though you will be working with various tools, gardening includes some hand pulling of weeds. The thorns may be included and you will need to protect your hands from scratches. If you are working with the soil directly, it will not only get you dirty, but it may dry your skin up. This is another great reason to purchase good gardening gloves. And finally, any excessive work done with the tools can cause blisters on your skin, so gloves

will protect you from that provided they fit your hands perfectly. Size does matter because if the gloves are loose, they will promote the blisters instead of preventing them. Choose the gloves well, the material needs to offer enough protection but allow your skin to breathe. Many people buy plastic gloves in which their hands get sweaty and it becomes very difficult to work with. There are materials out there that are hard and durable but also light and will allow circulation of the air.

2. **Pruning shears** come in several types and you will be choosing the ones that best fit your needs. Anvil pruners work just like a knife on a board where the sharp knife edge meets the flat surface. These are excellent when you need to cut off deadwood. However, if you use them on plants that are still alive, you may cause some damage. For live plants, you would need bypass pruners which will leave a clean cut without much damage. You will be using pruning shears quite often, especially after the harvest season is over and you need to clean up your garden. Because of the amount of work, pruning shears can cause some hand or wrist pain, especially if you are suffering from arthritis. However, you may want to opt for ratcheting pruners as they provide increased cutting strength.

The ratchet is an extra mechanism the pruners might have to make the difficult cutting much easier.

3. **Loppers** are long-handled pruners with which you will be able to cut thicker branches or to reach the places that would be otherwise hard to get to. The long handle offers extra leverage, making the cutting with loppers very easy. Just like with the pruners, loppers can be anvil or bypass and they serve the same purpose as described above. The longer the handle, the easier the cutting will be. But remember that a longer handle means extra material. These will be extra heavy. Think about what you will cut with loppers. If you need to cut tree branches, you might want to opt for longer handles, but if you need to trim bushes and softer plants, shorter handles will do just fine. They usually vary from 12 to 36 inches.

4. **Garden fork** is a very versatile tool. Their intention is turning soil, but they can be more efficient than a spade at digging the clay and very hard earth. They are also good at scooping and spreading mulch and turning compost. You can even use them as pitchforks to scoop dry or fresh grass cuts and fallen leaves. There are two different types of garden forks: with straight tines which are

good for digging, and with a slight curve to the tines which are great for turning over the soil or compost. If you are using the garden fork for digging and turning the soil, choose ones with square rather than flat tines as they will be more resilient if they hit a rock or a hard root.

5. **Hand trowels** are used most often during the early seeding and planting season. They are an essential tool for every gardener as the uses for them are almost endless. You will use them to transplant seedlings, dig out the weeds, or clear the earth around the plants. Choose the stainless steel hand trowels because you will often hit rocks and hard earth with it while digging out your plants, or while clearing the weeds. They come in two basic shapes: wide-headed which is great for moving and scooping the soil, and long and thin-headed which will serve you better for digging out the weeds. Hand trowels may also come with sharp blades at the end. This type is known as tulip trowels and the blades can cut through stubborn roots of the weed with ease. They can also be used for digging and turning the soil if needed.

6. **Spade** is one of the best-known gardening tools. It comes with a short and long handle. While a long handle makes them heavier, it provides more

leverage and the work with it is easy. A spade is similar to a shovel, but its head is square-shaped. It is used for both digging and scooping. They are also used for edging and moving dirt from one area to another. They can be pricey, but the quality of a spade is what counts. You want a stainless steel head so it is durable and won't rust. The handle needs to be of ashwood so it absorbs the vibration but is also durable.

7. **Rakes** will be your best friend during the autumn. They are a tool that will help you scoop fallen leaves as well as other garden debris while you are preparing the soil for the winter. They come in various shapes and sizes, but for a beginner, a leaf rake is the best choice as the tool itself is versatile. Make sure the tines are sturdy, otherwise, you may break them if you use them for any other type of work around your garden.

8. **Hoes** come in many varieties and what you are growing in your garden will determine what type of hoe you need. The hoe for the veggie garden needs to be sturdy because you will use it to dig rows for planting the various vegetables. However, the flower garden will use a sharp and flat hoe which will allow you to easily cut the weed and remove it from the surrounding area of the flower

beds. The hoe needs to have a long, comfortable handle which will help you reach further places. It also needs to have a stainless steel head for its durability.

9. **Garden hose** is very important because its purpose is watering the plants. We already said how water is one of the essentials for strong and healthy plants. You want the garden hose to be long enough so you can reach all the corners of your garden without pulling it over the plants. This means you will have to go around various obstacles so you don't damage the crops. Because of this, the hose needs to be longer than the diameter of your garden. The best thing you could invest in when it comes to a garden hose is an adjustable nozzle. It will allow you to control the water pressure and spray radius. Hoses also need to be sturdy because the lighter ones can easily be damaged. When not in use, keep the hose out of the direct sunlight because it can melt it or create weak spots. Remember that the length of the hose will directly influence the water pressure and this is why the adjustable nozzle is amazing. It will allow you to lower the diameter of the exit point of the very long hose, increasing the pressure.

10. **Watering can** is mostly used in very small

gardens where the hose is not needed as every corner of all plant beds can be reached easily. It can be made of plastic or metal. Of course, the metal ones will last longer, and if you choose one, make sure that the metal is galvanized so it doesn't rust. The modern watering cans usually come with the adjustable neck so it can serve two purposes, sprinkling and pouring water which will depend on your plant's preference. They can also come with one handle or two handles, suitable for elder gardeners or children.

11. **A wheelbarrow** is a tool that will greatly help you with any type of work that involves moving things from one place to another. Wheelbarrows can serve you to move large amounts of soil, compost, mulch, or garden debris. However, you need to make sure you are taking good care of this tool if you want to use it with ease. Make sure the wheel is inflated enough, otherwise, it can be very hard to haul things. Also, clean and store wheelbarrows in a dry place to prevent rust.

Tools Maintenance

To keep your tools in good working condition, you will need to clean them, sharpen them, patch them up, and sterilize them. The cleaning will need to be done after each gardening session for the simple reason that tools can be contaminated with soil-borne plant diseases that you can spread around your whole garden. Fortunately, taking care of the gardening tools is very easy and it will only take you a few minutes to deal with. There are two main types of tool maintenance: daily and seasonal. Daily maintenance will be performed every time you work with the tools and you are done for the day. Seasonal maintenance will be performed only at the end of the season. If you took proper care of the tools during the planting and harvesting season and you stored them properly, there won't be much work around them in the end.

After each gardening session, rinse the tools to remove any dirt that is lingering on them. If there are hard chunks of dirt that won't be removed so easily, try using a brush or a wire. You can even use soapy water to make sure your tools are sterile enough and that possible bacteria and insects are removed from them. Don't forget that tools that were not used in dirt such as pruners, loppers, and shears need cleaning too. They might not look dirty, but if you used them to cut diseased parts of the plants, they may be carriers of microorganisms that will contaminate other plants in your garden.

If you are certain you worked with diseased plants, make sure to soak your tools in a solution of water and bleach.

This will get rid of all the nasty pathogens that could easily be spread around your garden. Mix 2 cups of household bleach with one gallon of water for this purpose, but don't forget to rinse the tools with clean water after. You can also opt for rubbing some alcohol on your tools to make sure all the bacteria are dead, but bleach has a wider range of pathogens it can kill. After washing, your tools need to be properly dried to prevent rust. For this purpose, you can either sun dry them or use a towel or any other cloth if there is not enough sun to quickly evaporate the extra water.

Metal parts of the tools should be given special attention as you want to protect them from rust. You can prepare a mixture of sand and vegetable oil. Sand should be damp with the oil, not completely wet. After you cleaned your tools, you can dip them in the oiled sand and store them in a dry place. The oil will keep your metal tools protected for a very long time. You might be wondering why you wouldn't just use machine oil, and why vegetable oil is necessary. This is because most of the machine oils use petroleum in their mixtures. Next time you use the tool for digging or moving the earth around, you will be contaminating the soil with petroleum.

When it comes to seasonal tool maintenance, it mostly involves deep cleaning. This means that tools need to be taken apart, if possible, and cleaned properly. Especially sheers, pruners, and loppers. Aside from regular cleaning in soapy water, you might want to remove any accumulated rust. For this, you will soak them in 1:1 solution of vinegar and water and then you will rub the tools using steel wool. Rinse your tools once more in soapy water and then in clean water. Dry them well and rub vegetable or mineral oil before storing them in a dry, well-ventilated space.

Tools also need to be kept sharp, especially tools used for digging, cutting, and shearing. If your tools are not sharp, they can damage the wood and break it. Clean cuts are more resilient to the bacteria and fungi while broken branches are more prone to catch a disease. You can choose to sharpen your tools yourself or take them to a professional. Some of them may be tricky to sharpen due to their specific shape. However, for most of them, quick use of a sharpening stone will be enough. Wear eye and hand protection while you are sharpening tools because you could hurt yourself if you mishandle them. They can also create sparks which would be dangerous for your eyes.

Wooden handles need attention too. If they are severely damaged, they can cause problems. Check the handles for cracks and damage occasionally. After each use, you can clean them with a damp cloth. As for seasonal maintenance of the wooden handles, you might want to clean them, sand them lightly, and add a thin layer of vegetable oil. The wood will soak this oil and it will act as a conditioner.

CHOOSING YOUR PLANTING SYSTEM

To choose the best planting system for your garden, you will have to take a few things into account, such as the size of your garden, the type of plants you want to grow, and the growing conditions you can offer to your garden. The goal is to provide the plants with the best and most useful way of gardening in order for them to grow healthy and strong. However, you will also want your garden to look attractive and to provide you with pleasure while you are working in it.

If you have a large backyard that you want to turn into a garden, you might want to consider a **traditional planting system**. However, this type of gardening demands lots of work and plenty of time to invest. To do it, you will need to clear your whole backyard of weeds and you will also need to dig it up and turn the ground. If the soil quality is not the best, you will add compost or any other organic matter source to the whole yard. Only then can you decide where you should plant what exactly and make a footpath in the center of the garden and in between the plots so you can approach the crops when needed.

If you want to be as ecologically aware as possible while gardening, consider **Permaculture**. This system of gardening focuses on work in balance with nature in which you are just a guest. You will want to reduce, reuse, and recycle in order to decrease your carbon footprint. The idea of permaculture is to let nature do what it does best so you won't have to labor around your garden. This means extra planning where and how to plant your crops. You will have to measure all factors: the sun, the water, the quality of the soil as well as shade, moisture, and wind, to know what to alter and what to plant. Permaculture also demands no use of chemicals, including organic pesticides and fertilizers. You will have to use compost bins, water butts, and wormeries in order to minimize the garden waste. Although it sounds like much more work, once everything is settled, you won't have to do much labor tending to your garden because nature will do most of the work. Permaculture can be applied to any garden size and it can be very efficient even for the smallest ones.

Digging is really hard work but it is also a perfect ground for weeds to grow. Soil that has been dug out will dry more easily and the crops will have reduced exposure to moisture. Because of this, some gardeners developed a **no-dig method**. No-dig means you will need to construct wooden boxes that will hold the planting beds in place. They will need to be at least 6 inches high (15cm) and hammered into the ground with pegs. Then you will prepare the soil by covering it with a layer of newspapers, sawdust, straw, and grass clipping mulch. On top of that, you will add a layer of compost. To finish your planting beds for a no-dig method, you will add around 2.5 inches (6cm) of soil. This will be your last layer in which you will plant the seeds. Over time, the planting bed will drop down because the layers of mulch and compost will be dissolved. You will also have to add a layer of compost on top of the soil periodically. The no-dig method is perfect for small gardens that don't require much work.

Raised beds work on the same principle as the no-dig method, but the planting beds are much taller. This is because the layer of compost needs to be thicker to ensure the fertility of the soil. Raised beds are amazing when it comes to dealing with bad quality soil which is poor in nutrients and has really bad drainage abilities. The box constructed for the raised bed can remain wooden, but it can also be made out of more permanent materials such as bricks. Raised beds are usually larger than the ones used for no-dig methods. However, much of your garden's space will be taken by the paths you walk on to approach your crops. This doesn't necessarily need to be a disadvantage. Maybe you will have less planting space, but the soil will remain soft because you won't be stepping on it. If you plan your raised beds well, you can provide them with coverage for colder days which can easily be deconstructed during the warm days. Otherwise, you can plant flowers on the outside edges of the raised beds to add the attractiveness to your garden.

Square foot gardening is the best system for very small gardens and a lack of space. It is similar to raised beds that will be divided into a foot module in which you will plant each of your crops. This method of gardening is good for lettuce, salad vegetables, miniature vegetables such as cherry tomatoes, or herbs. Because the crops will be planted close to each other, they will create a microclimate suitable only to them. Weeds will not exist in square foot gardens. Because the foot module planting beds are easily accessible and low maintenance, you might enjoy this method of gardening, especially if you are a very busy person. This method will allow you to present healthy, organic food for your family, and still have free time to enjoy with them.

All the systems described above can be combined to make the best possible garden you will enjoy. You might plant vegetables the traditional way in one part of the garden while growing herbs in square foot planting beds near your house. For the best possible results, only you can decide how to combine the planting systems to improve the yields of your garden as well as to make it enjoyable to work in.

LEAVE A 1-CLICK REVIEW

Customer reviews

★★★★★ 4.5 out of 5

497 customer ratings

5 star		75%
4 star		13%
3 star		6%
2 star		2%
1 star		3%

˅ How does Amazon calculate star ratings?

Review this product

Share your thoughts with other customers

Write a customer review

I would be incredibly thankful if you could just take 60 seconds to write a brief review on Amazon even if it is just a few sentences. Go to https://amzn.to/31ZhZ0M or scan the code below, please.

CONCLUSION

The purpose of this book was to teach you the basics of organic gardening, so you can enjoy producing your own crops and serve them with pride to your friends and family. There is nothing more fulfilling than growing your own food, preparing it, and watching the smiling faces of your loved ones who will appreciate all the work that went into it. However, there is no such book out there that can take all the hard work of gardening away from your shoulders. Work simply must be done and there is no better person to do it but you! After all, it is all about your organic garden.

But through working with soil, you will gain more and more experience. You will learn the behavior of the plants you are trying to grow, what they like, and what they don't. What makes them thrive and what kills them easily. Learning gardening from a book is the smallest fraction of the needed knowledge, but it is the one that counts the most as it comes just before the start of the garden. All the other knowledge you will need about gardening will come in time, through your hard work.

Now you know how to test the soil, how to fertilize it properly, and what signs of life to look for. You know how to measure the sunlight, the shade, the drainage of the soil, and its pH values. All these things will give you a great advantage compared to people who start gardening with no information at all. If you are lucky, sticking a seed into the ground may be enough and something will germinate out of it. But gardening is so much more than that. Your plant is like a child, it needs proper care in order to thrive. No matter if you want to grow vegetables, herbs, or flowers, the love and care you pour into the soil will be answered.

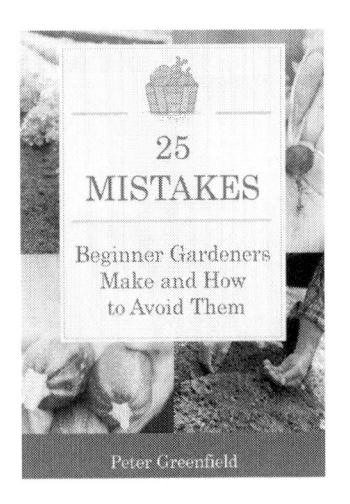

A Free Gift Just for You!

Download this free ebook to ensure you are not making any of those mistakes that could jeopardize your hard work. Click the link below.

Do not start your garden without reading this ebook.
Download the Free ebook
https://bit.ly/25-mistakes

Want access to a private community of passionate gardeners?

Being around like-minded people is the first step in being successful at gardening.

Join us and be part of an amazing community of gardeners just like you and share your experiences, stories, pictures and questions.

JOIN US!
https://bit.ly/backyardGardenerCommunity

REFERENCES

All images obtained from Pixabay.com.

United States Department of Agriculture, Office of Information, Radio Service. (1939). *Garden pests*. Washington, D.C.

Hellyer, A. G. L. (1966). *Garden pests and diseases: a guide to recognition and control*. London: Collingridge.

Lawton, B. P. (1992). *Improving your garden soil*. San Ramon, CA: Ortho Books.

McCampbell, S. C. (1942). *Vegetable crop pests*. Fort Collins, CO: Colorado State College, Extension Service.

McMaugh, J. (2018). *What garden pest or disease is that?: organic and chemical solutions for every garden problem.*

Chatswood, NSW: Reed New Holland Publishers (Australia).

Place, G., & Reberg-Horton, C. (2008). *Rotary hoe: a blind cultivation tool for in-row weed control*. Raleigh, NC: N.C. Cooperative Extension Service.

Manufactured by Amazon.ca
Bolton, ON